MW00978473

Down a Country Lane

...to a closer walk with God

Dene Ward

for your journey

Down a Country Lane
© 2017 by DeWard Publishing Company, Ltd.
P.O. Box 6259, Chillicothe, Ohio 45601
800.300.9778
www.deward.com

Cover by Albrecht Design.

Reasonable care has been taken to trace original sources for any excerpts and quotations appearing in this book and to document such information. For material not in the public domain, fair-use standards and practices were followed. Should any attribution be found to be incorrect or incomplete, the publisher welcomes written documentation supporting correction for subsequent printings.

Printed in the United States of America.

ISBN: 978-1-936341-95-5

For Tom and Helen Hill

and

Wayne and Glenda Smith

good neighbors for more than three decades

Dedication

Neighbors are different out in the country. First of all, they are a whole lot further away. Instead of zero lot line houses barely five feet away they are 5 to 50 *acres* away. You seldom even see one another to wave, except maybe at the lineup of mailboxes out on the highway. In the country, if you want to see your neighbors, you have to make it happen.

In the city a good neighbor often boils down to this: he's quiet and doesn't cause any trouble. In the country, because you are so far out of town and away from help, "neighbor" takes on a much larger meaning. The very lifestyle means you have far more need of one another.

You pull one another's vehicles out of the mud with a 4x4 or a tractor.

You feed one another's livestock and milk the goats when the other one has to be out of town a few days.

You tag team generators when the power goes out for more than a couple of hours, which happens far more often than in the city. You get the generator till noon, then loan it out for four hours to get your neighbor's freezer cooled back down before he gives it back, and so on around the clock.

You swap garden tilling for tractor mowing and tomatoes for blueberries.

You help one another shell peas and shuck corn, and then work together one hot afternoon to get it all put up.

You help load 100+ pound sick or injured pets into the pickup bed for an emergency run to the vet.

You trade shooting lessons for help wiring the shed.

You dig ditches when an access road is swamped and your neighbor cannot get home.

If a widow is alone, you load up her woodstove and get it set, ready to light on a cold night. If a husband is away and there is a household emergency—like the refrigerator door falling off!—you head down the lane immediately and screw it back on.

When a well collapses and can't be fixed for several days, you rinse out your towable tank and fill it with water so at least the bath water won't need hauling, and leave the back door open so clean jugs and pitchers can be filled for drinking water whether you're home or not.

When a storm passes through and leaves a live oak half out of the ground leaning over a house, all the neighbors up and down the highway drop everything and run with their tractors, chains, and chainsaws to help.

There is something a little more primal about being a neighbor in the country.

The Hills* and the Smiths have been neighbors like that from the beginning and we've tried to be neighbors like that in return. I think it's the sort of thing Jesus had in mind when he told the story of the Good Samaritan. It isn't a matter of borrowing a cup of sugar. It isn't about keeping the TV low in the wee hours or not parking on someone else's property. It's about real life and death matters, real trials and suffering, and aiding in whatever way you can. They have and we appreciate it.

Dene Ward

---

*When this book went to the publisher, Tom and Helen Hill were still with us. However, they passed away the week of March 19, 2017, within days of each other. Tom was the first person we met that first day we drove down the country lane to see the property advertised out on the rural highway nearly 32 years ago. Our neck of the woods will have a huge hole in it now. They will be remembered for their neighborliness by our family and a great many more.

DOWN A COUNTRY LANE

1. Wading in the Water

We found this plot of land only because Keith drove down the highway one day and saw a sign pointing off to the east: FIVE ACRES FOR SALE BY OWNER. When he stopped he could barely tell that a trail led off the highway, over a shallow rise and on into the woods beyond. Being in the market for a place to put our home, we followed it one day, driving carefully over a bumpy track and eventually onto a grassy downhill slope, hoping we would not bottom out in an unseen gopher hole or mushy spring. Half a mile later, we stood under some big old live oaks draped with Spanish moss, knee deep in grass and weeds, with an open field just over the pushed-up fence row. About a month later, this became home.

When you move onto unimproved land, you discover quickly the value of roads. Roads are built above the general lay of the land, usually ditched on the sides. A new neighbor, who has become a good friend, suggested that we have the septic tank man scrape down the fence row behind the house, which left a path several feet above the rest of the land. We did not use it, instead driving across the top of the property on the grass to the front door. The summer rains began shortly after we moved in, followed by a nearby hurricane, and after having another neighbor pull the car out of the mud with his tractor at least three times, we began using the raised fence row as our driveway. That is why to this day, you pull up to the back of the house instead of the front.

Another problem lay just a couple hundred feet off the highway—a low spot you never noticed until it rained four or five inches. Overnight the land around it drained and made a pond between us and the road. There was no way to go around because of the neighbor's fences, and the low spot was a bowl that could not empty. For a couple of months in August and September, we parked by the highway, waded through the pond, and walked the rest of the half mile to the house.

Sundays were particularly interesting. We all dressed the top half of ourselves, then put on shorts, and carried towels. After walking to the offending body of water, we waded through slowly, careful not to splash mud on the Sunday clothes above our waists, then got into the car, dried off, and finished dressing. When we came home, we reversed the process. Returning from evening services was particularly thrilling, hoping nothing deadly swam by us in the knee deep water and using flashlights to make sure we didn't step on any snakes as we trudged to the house in the dark, with buzzing mosquitoes for company.

Keith worked for years on that spot. An acquaintance did roofing and often had piles of old gravel that needed to be hauled off. Keith would stop by his work site in the evenings, load gravel into his pickup bed with a shovel he always had, bring it home and unload it before coming back to the house. There must be a good three feet of gravel beneath the dirt there now, for fifty feet along that low spot. Eventually he dug a ditch off to the side all the way to the highway, using nothing but a shovel, a two hundred foot long ditch, in places hip-deep, so the water would drain. Finally, we could count on getting through, regardless how much it rained. The people who have moved in have no idea how much they owe him.

I remember thinking, especially as I struggled to put on pantyhose in the front seat of the car, or as I fearfully followed the bouncing beam of a flashlight through the north Florida woods at night, that I had better not ever hear anyone else's excuses for not assembling with their brethren.

But I also remember this—not a single time did we even see (or hear) a snake on those scary evenings. Before that, when we could drive through, we saw several, even rattlesnakes and cottonmouths, but nothing on any pedestrian return trip from evening services.

Not a single time did we have to make that half mile walk in the rain. Certainly it had rained beforehand or the pond would not have been there, and often it rained more after we returned home, but we never got wet on our walks. Yes, that was a trying time, but it could have been worse. God knew what we could handle and He expected us to do just that—handle it. In return, He took care of us and never allowed it to be more of a burden than we could overcome.

Too many times we view our troubles from the wrong side and fail to see God's helping hand. Even when we think otherwise, He is there, guiding us and making things bearable. Sometimes we won't realize that till long after the trial is over. Remember that the next time a difficulty arises. I guarantee that as long as you are faithful, God is too, and one of these days you will see that as clearly as through a newly cleaned window.

We have had many difficulties since then, but I find myself looking back on what now seems minor compared to our more recent problems. If we had not waded through the water, if we had not followed a flashlight through the woods, could we have made it through what came after? Probably not, and a wise Father knew that. I find myself thinking, God, can I please have another pond to wade through? But the days of puddles are past. Rivers lie ahead, and we know we can get across them now, in part because of a muddy pond twenty-five years ago.

Be free from the love of money, content with such things as you have; for He has said, I will in no way fail you, nor in anyway forsake you. So with good courage we say, The Lord is my helper; I will not fear; what shall man do to me?

Hebrews 13.5–6

2. The Country Lane

Our piece of property was once a watermelon field on the back side of a family farm, approached by a dirt lane a half mile long. When we first drove onto it, the ground was furrowed under the waist high grass and weeds, and a pushed up wind row ran down the length of it parallel to the north property line. A few volunteer vines wound their way through the weeds, laden with green-striped melons, most of them too small to even consider picking. What the land had once been was obvious.

It had served other purposes as well. After we moved onto the property, the power company sent a crew to plant the poles and string the wires that would connect us to the outside world. One of the young men looked around and said, "I know this place. I went to school with one of the boys and we'd come back here to hunt rat—." Instantly he stopped and muttered, "Well—you don't need to know that." But within a week we knew exactly what he had started to say as the evidence began to pile up. That first summer we killed four rattlesnakes, the *smallest* of which was four feet long, two cottonmouths, and several coral snakes.

The snake population has dwindled after all these years, and the only volunteer melons come up in the garden now. But there is still more evidence of the property's past.

When we moved here, our closest neighbor advised us to have the wind row scraped into a raised road so we would always have access, even in wet weather, very good advice as it turned out. What the tractor left behind was a high, compact, dirt driveway, but it was littered with broken glass. Someone had tossed quite a few beer bottles into the wind row—those boys were obviously doing more than hunting rattlesnakes on the back forty all those years ago. That first summer we gave our boys, who were then 6 and 8, a nickel for every piece of glass they picked up, and it was soon safe to drive and walk on.

Yet now, over thirty years later, as I walk down the drive with the morning sun shining on the sandy road, I still see it glinting off tiny pieces of glass. The sand they have been buried in has worn off their sharp edges making them far too smooth to endanger either tires or bare feet. I usually pick up a couple dozen every summer. Then the next year, yet more will have worked their way to the top from the simple erosion of wind and rain.

What is hidden beneath will always come out. No matter how hard you try to hide the ugliness, something will always give it away. "By their fruits you shall know them," Jesus said, and, "Out of the heart the mouth speaks" (Matt 7.20; Luke 6.45). When we try to hide our character flaws from others, the only person we really manage to hide them from is ourselves.

God will help you overcome the weaknesses that beset you, but he cannot do it until you admit them to yourself, and then to Him. Blaming others, blaming circumstances, blaming "the way I am" will never fix things, any more than me blaming those teenage boys for throwing their beer bottles got rid of the glass in my driveway. But God can help you mend your heart and correct your ways. He promises He will always supply a way of escape and strength to endure the times of stress and the simple erosion of life that make those ugly things rise to the surface.

Every year I see those sparkly pieces of glass in the driveway, but their edges have worn smooth and they are no longer a danger. God can help the same way. You may feel something inside begin to rise to the surface, but with His help you can keep it under control so that it no longer hurts you or others. In your surrender to Him, the strength you have will multiply beyond anything you have ever experienced, or could ever have imagined.

> *Little children, you are from God and have overcome them, for he who is in you is greater than he who is in the world.*
>
> 1 John 4.4

3. Let's Take a Walk

Over the years I have found that I do my best thinking when I am walking Chloe around the property. Often I get my strongest prayers in then too. I can speak out loud without worrying about being overheard by anyone but God, and Chloe, of course, who doesn't seem to mind a bit. Occasionally she even looks over her shoulder and give me an encouraging tail wag to let me know so.

I thought today I would take you on our daily walk. When I do my thinking, I often ramble a bit, and so this will be "rambling while we ramble." I hope it will help you as much as it does me to clarify my thinking, to remind myself of basic truths, and to meditate on the things I have always known in order to find newer, deeper truths.

The East Side of the Path

Keith has mown a path for me, as safe as a path can be for someone with my eyesight, so I can walk Chloe, our Australian cattle dog, at least one lap every day with the trekking poles for balance and stability. Elliptical machines are great for low impact aerobics, but you don't get any fresh air and the scenery never changes. With this path I get the best of both. Let me take you for a stroll, beginning with the east side.

When I come out and slip on my walking shoes, Chloe, always waiting expectantly under the porch, bounces out and sits impatiently on the steps, her ears tall and her eyes never leaving me. "Just a minute," I tell her, and she seems to have grown to recognize those sounds. She knows I will indeed be outside shortly, but I wonder if her doggy brain wonders about people having to put on their feet before they come outside? Sometimes she cannot abide the wait, especially if I have to do more than put on my shoes—like spot Keith as he lifts weights on the other end of the porch—so she gives just a tiny little whine, so anxious she shimmies across the boards on her rear end.

As soon as I open the door she is halfway through it. We cannot go anywhere or do anything until she gets a pat on the head. Then I say, "Let's go walk," and she heads toward the morning sun peeking through the woods to the east, dappling the ground where we walk. Often she has to stop and wait for me to catch up, but as soon as I round that first corner she is off again, inspecting every mound of dirt, every dew-heavy hanging shrub, every disturbed pile of leaves at the fence bottom.

Occasionally she will stop and stare through the fence to the property on the other side, heavily wooded, vines snaking up and through the oaks, pines, maples, and wild cherries. Just over the fence lies the run. We thought it was a creek when we first moved here, a shallow one but water always sat in the bottom, slowly draining to the south. Then we went through the drought of the nineties and learned differently. It's a run. Whenever rain comes through, the land on all sides of us for at least a half mile in every direction, runs into that narrow, deep channel and heads for the swamp a mile to the south. After a typical summer afternoon downpour the water will rush loudly, white water at the bends and at every drop, carrying with it leaves and limbs shed by the overhanging branches.

You do not realize how powerful water moving downhill can be until you see the aftermath. We came out one morning to find the trash can washed up against the south fence, the run itself clear of all debris, and the pigs in the southeastern pigpen a pinky white they hadn't been since they were born. Only a small circle in the center of their backs remained black and muddy. Good thing they managed to find a high spot so they could get their noses up out of the draining water that had rushed over the banks of the run, gushing through the fence and cutting across the southeast corner of the property through their pen. We had no idea the water could rise that high.

The power of water is a constant theme in the Bible. We completely misunderstand 1 Peter 3.20–21, especially when we read the newer translations that make water not something that saves, but something to be saved from. Leave your new version a moment and look at the old ASV translation: "…the longsuffering of God waited in the days of Noah, while the ark was a preparing, wherein few, that is, eight souls, were saved through water: which also after a true likeness doth now save you, even baptism…." The waters of the flood saved Noah by bringing him and his family safely out of a world of sin, into a new world, one that was washed pure and clean. Baptism does the same for us. It saves us from the world of sin we live in, raising us to a new life free from sin—a chance to start over, this time with help from above. It also washes away the detritus of our old lives, if we let it, if we are willing to let go of the baggage and surrender all to the Lord.

Water had saved the Israelites in a similar way. They were "baptized" in the cloud and in the sea, walls of water on the side, a roof of vapor overhead. And then with a whoosh of water, God destroyed their enemies and set them in a new world, one where He and they were to enjoy a covenant relationship (1 Cor 10.1ff).

Amos uses water to symbolize the power found in justice and righteousness. Israel thought that multiplying sacrifices and feasts and other religious observances was all that mattered. God would be pleased, especially if the prescribed rites were even more elaborate than commanded. Then their lives during the rest of the week wouldn't count against them. The prophet told them differently, "Let justice roll down like water and righteousness like a mighty stream" (5.24).

That is just a small sample of the passages using water as a symbol. Spend some time today, as I did on my walk with Chloe, meditating on the simplest drink known to man.

> *Behold, God is my salvation; I will trust, and will not be afraid; for Jehovah, even Jehovah, is my strength and song; and he is become my salvation. Therefore with joy shall ye draw water out of the wells of salvation. And in that day shall ye say, Give thanks unto Jehovah....*
>
> Isaiah 12.2–4

The South Side of the Path

When we hit the corner we turn right along the south fence, just behind the old pigpen. We haven't had pigs since the boys left home—it would take the two of us a couple of years to go through a whole pig, but with teen-aged boys we managed easily in just a few months. Pork chops, ribs, hams, sausage, bacon, bacon, and more bacon. They grew up pork lovers and are to this day.

Yes, we named our pigs. We always called the males Hamlet, and the females Baconette, except the year we had two boys and the extra one we named Ribster. It reminded us from the beginning why we had them, and trust me—by the time a pig is ready for slaughter it isn't cute any longer. It is about as disgusting a creature as you can imagine. Slaughtering it was never a problem. The boys understood early on that we needed these animals to survive and respected them for it.

Just across the south fence and past the pigpen stands a live oak grove, a peaceful shady retreat we often wished had been on our property instead of the neighbor's. He has built a fire ring surrounded by several chairs, with a wood rack between two trees. He planned outings with his children and cook-outs with his friends and quiet evenings with his wife. He planted some Australian cypresses along the fence and now, after nearly ten years, they finally conceal his leafy sanctuary, a sanctuary he rarely visits any longer because his children are grown and living hundreds of miles away with all of his grandchildren. I doubt he used his beautiful spot more than half a dozen times. His wife passed unexpectedly several years ago. He has rebuffed friendly overtures and declined invitations to church. We seldom see him any longer, and there hasn't been even a lonely fire in the fire ring for three or four years. So much for great plans.

Chloe and I walk along that line of cypresses, peeking through the limbs sometimes, but usually watching the bottom of the fence line instead. Up ahead of me as usual, Chloe will occasionally stop and sniff around and when I reach her, sure enough, there is a depression in the ground where something slid under the fence during the night. Possums, coons, foxes, terrapins, sometimes we come across them during the day, but usually not. The depressions are well worn and even if we fill up the hole, it will be back within a couple of days, or a new one will show up just a few feet down the fence line. Interlopers will always find a way, and I can always tell from Chloe's attention and sniff pattern whether something more dangerous has slunk under or not.

That's exactly why God gave us elders, because "fierce wolves will come in among you, not sparing the flock" (Acts 20.29). Peter warns about false teachers who will infiltrate with "destructive heresies" (2 Pet 2.1). Jesus himself warned about "false prophets who come to you in sheep's clothing but inwardly are ravenous wolves" (Matt 7.15). Let me tell you, sheep are just as stupid as pigs are disgusting. We are too easily led astray, and once they get us away from our shepherds we are just as easily eaten up.

Our shepherds have a difficult job. They deserve our respect. They spend all hours of the day and night protecting us from things we do not even recognize as dangerous. Like Chloe, they see potential problems we in our ignorance and inexperience miss and all they get for it is accusations about traditionalism, legalism, and cynicism. We can make their job easier by spending more time in the word so we can recognize false teaching; more time with our brethren so we can share practical knowledge; and more time in safe places instead of hanging around the fence line in the dark of night where the wolves are always waiting.

Beloved, do not believe every spirit, but test the spirits to see whether they are from God, for many false prophets have gone out into the world.

1 John 4.1

The West Side of the Path
About two-thirds of the way across the south side of the property, the path cuts across diagonally to the west side. This avoids the wooded, tangled corner we have left that way for the wildlife—at least until all the townies moved out. That corner used to be a habitat for deer, turkeys, quail, foxes, armadillos, and warrens of rabbits, along with a bobcat or two passing through. The quail and the foxes have disappeared, the rabbits have thinned out—if you can imagine such a thing—and about all we have left are the occasional turkey and deer. I suppose nothing will ever rid us of the armadillos and possums.

On the inside of that section where the cut-off turns north to the driveway, stand four live oaks all growing out of the same spot. I am not certain if it is one huge tree with four large trunks or four smaller trees that have finally grown into one. Lucas and Nathan called it "the fort." Growing up they played in, on, and around it. You can climb up between the trees on a sort of ledge that hooks them together, and climb my little guys did.

The "fort" was not always a fort. Sometimes it was a castle, sometimes it was a spaceship, sometimes it was a hideout, but it was always a source of imaginative entertainment for little boys who didn't have a whole lot else except sticks and roots shaped like pistols, rifles, ray guns, phasers, and bazookas—at least to them.

This past year my grandsons Silas and Judah finally reached the age that they could enjoy the fort. Uncle Lucas got them started, showing them how to turn ordinary bark, sticks, and tree knots into weapons, controls, and push buttons. Now they clamber all over that same clump of giant oak trees, grown even closer together now that they are older, with even more ledges and platforms to stand on and jump off. It feels good to walk by that old favorite spot of my boys and know that a new generation is enjoying it too.

This will probably be the last generation of Wards to know the magic of that special spot. Neither of the boys is in a position to move back to this acreage and we will probably reach a point where we can no longer take care of it before the new generation even grows to adulthood. We will need the money it brings to buy us a smaller, easier place to live.

Think about that the next time you assemble with your brethren. I don't mean think about how the next generation will use the building or whether they will understand the sacrifices made to build it, the men who made it their business to watch over the construction, the women who furnished the classrooms and dolled up the restrooms the way men would never even think to. Think about what goes on in that building. When all of the older generation is gone, the ones who fought the battles and stood for truth no matter how unpopular it was, will the younger generation even know what that truth is? Will they understand the thought processes that produced a generation of faithful men and women?

Maybe some other family will someday own our land and figure out what that group of live oaks "really" is even with no one to tell them, but somehow I doubt that a generation so used to the here and now of social media and the pizzazz of loud, splashy entertainment that leaves no room for imagination will even have a clue. Tell them it's a spaceship and they will likely look at you like you're nuts.

Far more important is to be able to tell the next generation of Christians that "this"—whatever this is at the moment—is truth, and have them comprehend its importance.

> *You then, my child, be strengthened by the grace that is in Christ Jesus, and what you have heard from me in the presence of many witnesses entrust to faithful men who will be able to teach others also.*

> 2 Timothy 2.1–2

The Gate

We have reached the northwest corner where the gate opens onto our property and leads guests down the narrow drive, past the wild corner, a shady field, the grapevines, the jasmine, and between two azaleas that stand as sentries to our yard.

Thirty years ago we didn't have a gate, or a fence to attach it to. The titles on the land parcels back here off the highway were not free and clear, except for ours, so our boys grew up wandering over twenty acres in every direction. They swam in the run and climbed trees in the groves that now stand on other properties. They hunted and explored, and we cut our Christmas trees from the uninhabited woods around us.

Then the titles were cleared up and people began buying and moving in. Suddenly we had to deal with neighboring cows breaking through their fences and wandering our way to find good grass to eat, with pot-bellied pigs rooting in our garden, with donkeys braying loudly outside our windows, and packs of stray dogs terrorizing ours. So we scraped up the money we had been saving over the years and put in a fence, with the gate at the road we had driven down long before anyone even knew there was a road there. Now we can protect what is ours from wandering livestock, and the lock on the chain is especially nice during political season.

The gate is a two-banger. The larger portion is a standard cow panel, 16 feet wide. But that isn't enough space for a tractor pulling a cultivator and sprayer, which an old friend uses to plow and treat our garden once a year. So right next to the larger gate is a smaller one opening from the middle that adds four feet and just enough room for the equipment to come through.

Jesus had some things to say about wide gates and narrow gates. One thing I have noticed about wider gates. It isn't just that more people can get through them. It's that they can get through quickly. Narrow gates stay that way because they are seldom used, and when you see one, the very smallness of it makes you hang back and consider. Maybe you'll poke your head through trying to make out what's down there, but it still takes considerable thought before you will go down a place that not only few go, but they don't go quickly.

Wide gates on the other hand? People go through them in a headlong rush simply because everyone else does. Someone famous wears a certain color and before two weeks have passed everyone is wearing it. A celebrity eats at a certain restaurant and the next week there is a line a mile long. Someone posts a video on Facebook and it goes "viral." As soon as anything gets approval from a popular source, people can't get enough fast enough. It's a mania, a craze. Would you look at those words a minute? No thinking at all involved in those words, unless you classify insanity as a thought process. Jesus, on the other hand, expects his disciples to be thinkers.

Star Trek always starts with a prologue ending in these words: *to boldly go where no one has gone before.* Isn't that what Christianity is supposed to be? Except for this one, critical, factor: someone *has* gone before us. He tells us that yes, it's safe, at least in an eternal sense, and yes, you can do it too. The gate may be narrow and seldom entered, but that is what makes us special, something besides robots in a cookie cutter world.

Today take a moment to think before you choose. A quiet stroll with the Lord in a narrow shady lane may be just what your soul needs.

> **Enter by the narrow gate. For the gate is wide and the way is easy that leads to destruction, and those who enter by it are many.** *For the gate is narrow and the way is hard that leads to life, and those who find it are few.*
>
> Matthew 7.13–14

The North Side of the Path

And now we head east along the final leg, the north side of the property. We used to drive in that way, straight down the drive and across the top of the property to the front door. That was before we had a summer so wet we kept getting stuck halfway up our hubcaps. Somewhere along that north side is a spring that only appears during wet season and a neighbor had to pull us out of it with his tractor several times before we finally cleared a higher road we could count on that comes to the back door instead of the front. I keep telling people I would never put my washer and dryer in my foyer, but few seem to get it.

That wet weather helped us discover another problem. The property directly north of us drained all over us. We are on a slight grade, one you hardly notice until a summer downpour comes washing down from the neighboring land. I will never forget the day I stood at the front door and watched a six inch deep torrent rush under the house, then raced to the opposite windows to see it come churning out. I knew we were in big trouble. The summer rains had barely begun and we were also in the middle of hurricane season. In short order we would be washed away.

We have a law, at least here in Florida, which says you are responsible for what your property does to neighboring property. One of the neighbors found out the hard way when they did something on their property that left another neighbor in an undrainable, and un-drivable, swamp. The ones who caused the situation refused to fix it. "It's not our problem," they said. The neighbors who could no longer access their home had to call the sheriff, who sent out deputies to tell those selfish folks, "It is too your problem—you caused it," and to make them repair the mess so their neighbors could once again get in and out of their land.

The owners of the land just north of us, people who had bought it as an investment and did not live there, knew about that law, too. All we had to do was make a phone call, and they sent out the equipment to dig a ditch along that north side that led straight to the run on the east where we started this walk, so their land could drain around us instead of through us. Yes, it was a law, but at least we didn't have to call the sheriff to get them to act. In fact, they were quite nice about it and did not leave until they were certain we were satisfied.

God has a law too. It goes like this: "Whoever causes one of these little ones who believe in me to sin, it would be better for him if a great millstone were hung around his neck and he were thrown into the sea" (Mark 9.42). Paul spent a couple of chapters in both Romans (14) and 1 Corinthians (8) telling us the same thing. Everything we do has an influence on people who see or hear us, whether we know they see or hear us or not.

I've heard people say things like, "I can do whatever I want to do. That's his/her problem." No, it isn't. It's your problem when you want to claim to be a disciple of Jesus but do not follow his example. "We who are strong have an obligation to bear with the failings of the weak, and not to please ourselves. Let each of us please his neighbor for his good, to build him up. For Christ did not please himself, but as it is written, 'The reproaches of those who reproached you fell on me'" (Rom 15.1–3).

We influence people for good or ill by what we wear, how we speak, how we react to others, especially the unkindness of others, and any number of other things. God expects us to be aware of how our speech and behavior effects the world, and not only that, to *care*.

Wouldn't it be a shame if the world had to call "the Sheriff" on us?

So then each of us will give an account of himself to God. Therefore let us not pass judgment on one another any longer, but rather decide never to put a stumbling block or hindrance in the way of a brother.

Romans 14.12–13

4. The Dead Possum

Possums, or more properly "opossums," can be a nuisance. They rummage in the garbage, they poke about in the shed, and they ramble into the garden destroying perfectly good melons with a bite or two out of each one. That is one reason we have dogs, and Magdi, our first Australian cattle dog, did better than any other at solving the problem. For a while we had to bury one every day; she must have come across some sort of Possumopolis out in the woods.

One morning Keith found yet another as he was leaving for work, but he was so late he had no time to properly dispose of it. It was my turn to do the honors. I have come a long way in 35 years of country life, but I still won't pick up a dead thing, even with big thick gloves. So I got the shovel.

I am glad my neighbors are not close. I stuck the shovel edge down by the possum and pushed, assuming it would just slide under the offensive creature so I could carry it out to the woods and let nature do the disposal work. Instead, the shovel just pushed the possum along. I tried again, and again, and again. Every time I pushed, the possum moved farther and I wound up following it in a circle around the field. This possum might as well have been alive it was making such a merry chase.

Meanwhile Magdi stood to the side. She looked at me like I was nuts, but she also looked at me like she would really like to have her possum back. Occasionally she lunged at the possum as I made the circle yet again passing her on the right. So there I was pushing a dead possum in a circle around the yard with a shovel, while yelling at the dog at regular intervals, like some sort of bizarre ritualistic dance.

I stopped, winded and frustrated, and found myself next to the oak tree across the driveway from the well. The answer struck me, if only I had the energy left. I pushed the shovel again. Again it pushed the possum, this time right against the tree and the tree held it there for me as the shovel slid beneath it. Success!

I lifted the shovel—and the possum rolled right off of it. Somehow I kept from screaming. Okay, I told myself. You have learned something. Possums are heavy and you have to hold the shovel handle tightly so it won't tip. I tried again, pushing the possum up against the tree and lifting the shovel, this time ready for the shifting weight. Now I just had to get it to the woods. It was a several hundred yard trip, and that possum at the end of the shovel got heavier and heavier.

About halfway there I knew I was not going to make it, so rather than let the thing drop in a clearing where there were no trees to push against, I carefully lowered the shovel to the ground. As much as I hated to, I had to move my hand farther down the handle, closer to the possum so the weight would be easier to manage. I did, and it was easier, so much easier I could even walk faster without being in danger of losing the possum.

I was already dressed for Bible class and did not want to traipse into the woods among the briars and brush, so I carefully pulled back on the shovel and slung with all my might. The possum slid off the shovel about five feet into the brush, not much further than the length of the shovel handle. By then, I was ready to call that a great success, and left it.

As shocking as it might sound, that is the way we treat God sometimes. Instead of rushing into His safe and loving embrace, we keep Him at arm's length. Like a teenager who is too embarrassed to act like he loves his parents, we are too embarrassed to let our love for God show to those around us. We don't want to look too weird, too strange, too "fanatical."

Early Christians were known for their good works. In fact, that is how they often gave themselves away to their persecutors. They looked and acted so differently from everyone else. No one else was kind and forgiving, even when mistreated. Would our godly behavior give us away under similar circumstances, or would it lump us in with the crowd because our religion has not "contaminated" our lives?

Even among ourselves we don't want to say things that might make people look at us askance. It's like the old joke where the new convert sits in the pews saying, "Amen," and "Praise God," only to have some older member take him aside and say, "Son, we don't praise God here."

God wants us close to Him. Think about that for a moment. Our awesome all-powerful Creator wants a relationship with us. He made an incomprehensible sacrifice to make it possible. Maybe we need to be shocked with this analogy, so we will wake up. When we keep Him at arm's length like something disgusting, we are treating God like a dead possum.

> *Wherefore also He is able to save to the uttermost them that draw near unto God through Him, seeing He ever lives to make intercession for them…Draw near to God and He will draw near to you.*

> Hebrews 7.25; James 4.8a

5. Eating with the Pigs

I don't need to tell you the story of the Prodigal, or Wasteful, Son. I am sure you have heard the lesson so many times you might shut this book if I tried. All I want you to think about this morning is the point that young man had to reach before he could truly repent. He had to hit rock bottom. He had to wake up and find himself completely alone with nothing but the pigs for company and the food he fed them for sustenance.

We raised pigs when the boys were still with us. Every fall we put a new one in the freezer and it kept us well fed for a year. But after raising them, I can say with authority that it was a brave man who first ate one. Leaning over to put the feed in the trough and coming face to face with a snorting, muddy, ugly, animal whose head was twice as big as mine, and who nose was always running and caked with a mixture of dirt and feed was nothing short of disgusting. I never had a bit of trouble come slaughtering day, despite the fact that we named them all—either Hamlet or Baconette, depending upon gender.

When we have sinned against God, we need to reach the point that young man did, bending over and finding himself face to face with a filthy, reeking, disgusting animal. We need to understand how low we have sunk. For some it may not take as much. Their "rock bottom" may be a realization that comes from private study and its conviction, or someone's chance comment in a Bible class that hits the mark. That may be enough to turn their hearts. But for the stubborn, the arrogant, and the foolish, it will always take more. They have to have their noses rubbed in the mud of the sty to realize that they are indeed eating with the pigs.

But we must not think this is only for those who have "left" and then returned. This needs to happen every time we sin, not just the "big ones." Why do you think those little sins keep plaguing us? Because we have never seen them as anything but "little." We have let our culture and our own pride keep us from comprehending the enormity of sin and what it does to our relationship with our God. Nothing that caused the death of the Son of God is "little." "For all have sinned and fall short of the glory of God" (Rom 3.23). We don't understand "glory" if we think that even the tiniest amount of sin can stand in its presence. We have to, in the words of Ezekiel, "remember your evil ways and your deeds that were not good, and *loathe yourselves* for your iniquities and your abominations" (36.31).

So the next time you pray for forgiveness, ask yourself first if you recognize how far you have fallen; if you understand that any sin is horrible; that even the tiniest sin, as men count them, makes you forever unworthy to stand in the presence of an Almighty God.

Ask yourself if you realize that you have been eating with the pigs.

> *For godly grief produces a repentance that leads to salvation without regret, whereas worldly grief produces death. For see what earnestness this godly grief has produced in you, but also what eagerness to clear yourselves, what indignation, what fear, what longing, what zeal, what punishment! At every point you have proved yourselves innocent in the matter.*
>
> 2 Corinthians 7.10–11

6. Smoke

I stepped outside a few weeks ago, another humid late summer morning, and noticed first that it was not quite as warm as it has been, perhaps 70–71 instead of the usual overnight lows of 76–80. A breeze soon picked up and Chloe quickened the pace to an excited romp as we walked around the fence line.

The birds enjoyed the morning as well, especially a red-bellied woodpecker that sat on the old corner post of the dog pen, singing his high pitched "chuck, chuck, chuck." A cardinal answered with "purty, purty, purty," and soon a blue jay joined in the chorus with his pretty wooden whistle rather than the usual ugly squawk. But by the time Chloe and I returned from the gate, the birds had stopped singing and smoke had begun to filter in. Someone was burning off a field or a brush pile nearby, and before long I had to go inside just to take a deep breath and clear my lungs.

Smoke has a way of taking over. You can't miss whatever smell it brings—acrid leaf fires, fragrant wood fires, aromatic barbecues, or the sad and awful smell of someone's home burning to the ground. Whatever the odor, it hangs around for a long time, sometimes pleasant, sometimes not.

My favorite reference to smoke in the scriptures is the one in Revelation 8.3–4: "And another angel came and stood at the altar with a golden censer, and he was given much incense to offer with the prayers of all the saints on the golden altar before the throne, and the smoke of the incense, with the prayers of the saints, rose before God from the hand of the angel." Just as smoke cannot be ignored, just as burning incense fills your nostrils to the point that any other smell is extinguished, our prayers rise to God in a way He cannot disregard. We mean that much to Him.

If you have ever been in a room where someone has lit a scented candle some time in the day, you know its odor lingers long after. In fact, I can smell mine just walking by the drawer where I keep them, even inside a plastic bag, never yet having been lit. Incense is even stronger. That smell will permeate the furniture and draperies. It will seep through the cracks under and around the doors and waft down the halls. That is the figure God chose to encourage us. Even in the midst of the horrible suffering those early Christians were about to endure, He told them, "Your prayers to me will not be ignored. I will smell them as intensely and constantly as one smells the smoke of incense. I will not forget you or what you have endured for my sake."

That promise stands for us as well. It is easy, as we endure trial after trial, to think that God has forgotten us, that He no longer hears our prayers. Yet our prayers rise like incense every bit as much as those first Christians' prayers. Why did He save that writing for us if it isn't true? He knew what they were about to endure, and that they must endure it, so He gave them the ultimate encouragement—I am still here; I am still listening; I am in control and all will be well in the end.

So how much smoke are you sending up to Him as you face your trials? How strong is that burning incense? Don't make it so weak that even God would miss it.

O Lord, God of my salvation; I cry out day and night before you. Let my prayer come before you; incline your ear to my cry! ... Let

my prayer be counted as incense before you, and the lifting up of
my hands as the evening sacrifice!

Psalms 88.1–2; 141.2

7. The Donkey and the Cow

My neighbor does not take good care of his livestock. The horses, donkeys and cows all have ribs that show through their skin and sores on their hides, unfortunately, just below the level that the animal control people consider criminal neglect, so they will not intervene. I often think to myself that I would like to see those people have to endure the same things as these animals and then decide if it is abuse or not, particularly after those poor creatures have broken through the fence yet again and we must dodge them as they wander the road looking for something to eat.. We have even thrown some of our garden refuse over the fence to try to help them out.

As I walked up to unlock the gate one morning for an expected visitor, a donkey and a cow stood just across the west fence. The donkey evidently saw a meal on the hoof, walked up to the cow and started chewing its left ear. The cow was not pleased with the situation and turned around. So the donkey started chewing its right ear. The cow yanked its head away and trotted off, with the donkey trailing behind. As soon as the cow stopped, the donkey headed straight for her head and grabbed an ear again. Once again the cow turned around only to have the other ear chomped on. She took off again. I watched this for nearly five minutes before the cow finally headed for the fencerow and quite purposefully stuck her head in a bush.

The donkey tried to get to an ear and found himself struck in the face by the limbs and branches of the wild myrtle and unable to get to the cow's ears. I am afraid I could not help myself—I laughed out loud and cheered for the cow. After a few minutes, the donkey gave up and left, trotting across the field straight for another cow, braying loudly as he went. I had to go about my own business then, but I assume that cow had success as well since, while I still see the outlines of ribs and spines, I have yet to see any of those animals earless.

Sometimes some braying donkey of a human comes along and tries to chew on our ears. I am afraid that too often we let him when we should be turning aside and, if he is persistent, finding a bush to stick our heads into. As long as there is a market for gossip and slander, there will be people to fill the need, and when we listen we are no better than they because we find pleasure in their sin.

Gossip can accomplish a lot, and none of it good. It can ruin friendships, break up families, divide churches, and permanently stain reputations. It has been going on since Satan, the "slanderer," told Eve that God was just a selfish tyrant who did not want to share. Look where that got all of us.

Today, when someone comes to you with the latest "dirt," find a bush and stick your head into it. Don't let that person chew on your ears. Sooner or later he will get the message and move on.

He who goes about as a tale-bearer reveals secrets; therefore company not with him who opens wide his lips.

Proverbs 20.19

8. The Apple Tree

My back and feet were aching and my hands cramped from peeling by the time I finished. The seals on the pint jars of apple butter popped and I started the clean-up of unused jars and lids, the large pot covered with sticky residue, and the measuring cups and spoons. Finally it was over.

The apple tree had borne far more than ever before. I had made several pies, a couple dozen muffins and a cake, and canned two dozen quarts of applesauce, a gallon of apple juice, a dozen pints of apple jelly, half a dozen quarts of apple pie filling, and finally a half dozen jars of apple butter.

As I stood over a sink full of soapy water I muttered, "I hope I never see another apple as long as I live." The next spring my apple tree died.

When it became apparent that we couldn't save the tree, Keith looked at me and muttered something about not really knowing what that might mean—the fact that I could curse a tree and it up and die for no obvious reason so soon afterward. Just exactly who, or what, was he married to?

The county agent saved my reputation. The tree was planted too close to an oak, he said. Oaks carry a disease that kills fruit trees, especially apples and peaches. Sure enough, we soon lost our peach tree too.

All these years later, the story came up again, and with it a new perspective. Here I had cursed a tree that bore too much, while the Lord cursed one that bore too little.

And seeing in the distance a fig tree in leaf, he went to see if he could find anything on it. When he came to it, he found nothing but leaves, for it was not the season for figs. And he said to it, "May no one ever eat fruit from you again." And his disciples heard it. And as they passed by it in the morning, they saw the fig tree withered to its roots. (Mark 11.13–14, 20)

You might do as I did at first and wonder why the Lord would expect to find figs when it wasn't fig season. Yet every commentator I read said that figs produce their fruit *before* they leaf out. When the Lord saw a fig tree fully leafed out, he had every right to expect to see some fruit, even if it was small and green. As a gardener I know that nearly every plant has at least one "early-riser"—a tomato or pepper or blueberry that ripens before the others. Even if there was nothing ripe, there should have been plenty of fruit hanging there, gradually ripening on the leafy branches.

Now how about us? Is anything ripening on our branches? Is the fruit of the Spirit perhaps still a little green, but nonetheless visible as we become more and more what he would have us be? Or are we nothing but leafy show: lots of pretty clothes on Sunday morning but behavior like the rest of the world throughout the week? Lots of talk in Bible class, but no good works in the community? Quoting catchphrases to our neighbors, but never opening the Book in our own homes? More concerned with winning arguments than winning souls?

The Lord will come looking for figs in our lives, more than likely at a season in which we are not expecting him. He told us we would recognize false teachers by their fruits (Matt 7.16–20). What will he recognize about us from ours or will there even be any for him to see?

And so, from the day we heard, we have not ceased to pray for you, asking that you may be filled with the knowledge of his will in all spiritual wisdom and understanding, so as to walk in a manner worthy of the Lord, fully pleasing to him, bearing fruit in every good work and increasing in the knowledge of God.

Colossians 1.9–10

9. The Mousetrap

It did not take long for this city girl to discover one common problem with country life—mice. One morning I walked out to the kitchen to discover that the dog had had a playmate all night, and it was lying right in the doorway to the kitchen, all "played" out. So we set out traps, especially in the large walk-in pantry/laundry area. If anything would attract the mice we figured it would be the warmth from the water heater and the food on the shelves.

The pantry shared a wall with the dining area. One frigid morning we were eating breakfast when we suddenly heard a sharp snap, followed by a thump on that wall's other side, then squeak, squeak, squeak, squeak, and a scrambling of tiny feet. I didn't think this was the way mousetraps were supposed to work, but what did I know? Before that fall, I had never even seen one except on cartoons.

Keith walked around, peered into the pantry, and started laughing. When we had set the trap inside the door, we had pushed it in with the peanut butter side against the wall and the spring on the side toward the door. Evidently the mouse had climbed onto the spring and when he started nibbling on the peanut butter, it had snapped, catapulting him into the wall. Having survived the trap, he had run away unscathed except, perhaps, for a nasty bump on the head.

That night we reset the trap, this time pushing it in the other way around. Sure enough, as we were eating breakfast the next morning we heard the snap, followed by a deathly quiet. Keith disposed of the interloper after we finished eating.

That mouse thought he had found a way around the trap. That dumb animal thought he was safe because one time he had had a nibble without it killing him. If mice could think such things, I could just imagine, "It won't happen to me," coming out of his mouth, just like a few dumb humans I know of. It isn't enough to stay out of the trap—you have to stay completely away from it. "Thorns and snares are in the way of the perverse; He who keeps his soul shall be *far from them*" (Prov 22.5).

Job pictures the life of the wicked as nothing but snares (18.8–10). Jeremiah says they lay snares for the righteous (5.26). How do they do that? By their very lifestyles. We look, and we want, and we wish, and suddenly we do—just like they do. God warned the Israelites not to even covet the gold and silver covering the idols, "lest you be snared therein" (Deut 7.25). It is not enough to just want their lives and "not do the sins they do—I know better than that!" How can we not eventually fall into the same things they did? Because, like that mouse, we think we have found a way to nibble on one side and not be caught by the other.

The Proverb writer says we are often ensnared "with the words of our own mouths" (6.2). We say we abhor sin, we say we don't want to do bad things, but with the same mouth we idolize people who live without morals, without integrity, and without self-control, people who care nothing at all about God. They may even wear crosses around their necks and thank the Lord in public, but they turn right around and profane Him with their lives. And we think we wouldn't be trapped by sin the same way they are? How foolish, how immature can we be?

Don't glamorize sin. Don't worship those who do. Don't make the mistake of thinking you can sit on one side of the mousetrap and have a bite of something good, and a fun, and exciting ride to boot. The next time you nibble, someone may very well have turned the mousetrap around.

> *But my eyes are toward you, O GOD, my Lord; in you I seek refuge; leave me not defenseless! Keep me from the trap that they have laid for me and from the snares of evildoers!*
>
> Psalm 141.8–9

10. Sun on the Pine Straw

It was one of those recuperating days I have had so many of the past few years, so I sat in my lounger outside, the early morning autumn breeze ruffling my hair, a sweet little dog snuffling for a pat at my side, looking out over our domain, such as it is. The east sun was filtering through the woods fifty yards in front of me, not yet high enough to cause me any trouble.

I had carried a pair of binoculars to do a little bird-watching, but saw on the northeast corner of the property what looked like a giant orange bloom. So I lifted those heavy lenses and got a surprise. The bloom did not really exist. What I saw was the sun shining on a clump of dried out pine straw hanging on a low, dead limb. I pulled down the binoculars and looked again. I much preferred the big orange bloom.

Then I started looking around and saw some more. The dull green leaves near the top of the tree glinted like small mirrors in the few rays of sun that had pierced through to them. Even the gray Spanish moss resembled icicles. I knew in a few minutes the effect would all be gone. The sun would have risen high enough not to perform these magic tricks. Still, it reminded me of something important.

All by myself I am nothing, I can do nothing, and I have nothing to hope for. But the light of the gospel changes everything. Through that light, we are able to see the glory of Christ and believe (2 Cor 4.3–6). When we are raised from the waters of baptism, God's glory gives us the power to walk "in newness of life" (Rom 6.4). We transform ourselves into the image of His Son by the renewing of our minds (Rom 12.2, 8.29). When the glory of the Lord shines on us through our submission to his gospel, what looks plain and ordinary becomes beautiful, what looks dead and repulsive becomes glorious. That's us we're talking about—you and me. We can be beautiful.

Look at your life today. Would someone see a beautiful bloom, a sparkling mirror, a glittering icicle? They only will if you have allowed that light inside you, if you have let it have its way, transforming you into the person God meant you to be from the beginning. Some will not do this. They fight it, and offer excuses of all sorts. "I'm only human after all." "No one is perfect." "Someone has to have common sense around here and not be such an innocent babe!" "It's my right after all." None of those will give anyone a beautiful view of a child of God.

Peter reminds us, "As obedient children, do not be conformed to the passions of your former ignorance, but as he who called you is holy, you also be holy in all your conduct, since it is written, "You shall be holy, for I am holy" (1 Pet 1.14–16). If we are not submissive to his will, we will never be transformed to his image. We will look like nothing but dried out pine straw on a dead limb, and all the excuses in the world will never change it.

"What would Jesus do?" may be an old denominational catch-phrase, but is it any different than, "Be ye holy as I am holy?" God desires nothing more than for us to be exactly like Christ, "conformed to the image of his son" (Rom 8.29), "that you might follow in his steps" (1 Pet 2.21). If you find yourself looking through the world's binoculars and seeing nothing but your old self, the light of the gospel has not reached your heart.

Conform yourself today. In every aspect of your life, in every action you take, and every word you speak, "be ye holy in all your conduct." You can do it, or God wouldn't have asked it of you.

> *But we all, with unveiled face reflecting as a mirror the glory of the Lord, are transformed into the same image from glory to glory, even as from the Lord the Spirit.*
>
> 2 Corinthians 3.18

11. Tornado Warning

About thirty years ago, we awoke one Saturday morning to ominous gray skies and strong winds. The forecast for the day made it dangerous to be out, so we called those we had invited for a singing that afternoon and canceled. Instead of walking to the paper box, about a quarter mile down our driveway, Keith drove the car, and as huge, plopping raindrops began falling, parked it next to the front door when he returned.

A few minutes later, he looked out the window by the table where he sat reading the paper and sipping a cup of coffee. Something in his manner made me look too, but I didn't see anything.

"Get the boys," he said very quietly, "and go crouch down in the middle of the house. Cover your faces." I did exactly as he said, unquestioningly. He grew up in the Arkansas mountains, and he knew about things I had no experience with. A few minutes later it was all over with. What "all" was, I still did not realize. The power had gone out, but we were still intact.

We stepped out of the house, and the hay barn across the field no longer had a roof. Several water oaks and wild cherry trees were down on the long drive to the highway. A large chinaberry had fallen right where the car had originally been parked before he decided to drive for the paper instead of walking. It would have been flattened.

Then we edged around the corner of the house on our bedroom side, and saw the worst of it. A huge live oak had split. Half had fallen on the power lines, but the line was still alive, wiggling and sparking on the ground. The other half, its roots mostly out of the ground, leaned right over our bedroom. We had no idea how long it would hold before it too fell and demolished our house.

We called the power company immediately and they rushed out to take care of the live wire, but they had too many other calls to send someone to handle the tilting tree. We would have to wait our turn. Word gradually spread down the highway, and within an hour, two men who worked timber drove up with cables and chainsaws, and those two men, who were complete strangers to us, took the tree down safely and with no damage. We thanked them profusely. "That's what neighbors are for," they said, and off they went.

A preacher friend who had been invited to the sing never got the message to cancel. He showed up amid the raucous roar of chainsaws, and heard the whole story. It impressed him enough to include it in a lesson on prayer and providence. The people in the audience were not impressed. Afterward they took him aside and scolded him. "God does not act in the world today," they reminded him. He was astounded, and so were we.

When we become so intent on exposing false doctrine that we blatantly ignore the truth, swinging the pendulum so far back that we miss it entirely, something is wrong with our perspective. If God had no hand in what happened that day, then why do we bother to pray at all? Do we not believe James?

"The effectual fervent prayer of a righteous man avails much" (5.16).

Do we not believe the book of Esther or the last 14 chapters of Genesis? "God sent me," Joseph told his brothers who had thought it was all their idea, and God continued to "send" Joseph through Potiphar's wife, the baker and butler, and eventually Pharaoh himself.

God spent much of the prophets talking about how He would work through the enemies of Israel. "Ho Assyrian! The rod of my anger! The staff of my fury is in his hand" (Isa 10.5). God sent those Assyrians to punish Israel, just as certainly as He sent those two lumberjacks to save my home. He did it because of the prayers I started the moment I saw that look in my husband's eye, the moment I crouched on the floor trying to shield my little boys with my own body, the moment we saw that tree clinging to the pitifully few clods of dirt left on its roots.

I will never believe otherwise. In fact, why do we bother if we don't believe it?

> *The LORD is near to all who call on him, to all who call on him in truth. He fulfills the desire of those who fear him; he also hears their cry and saves them.*

> Psalm 145.18–19

12. Finding the Smooth Way

It happens every time Keith and I walk the property. Suddenly I find myself pushed into the rough while he walks the path. I learned a long time ago to just push back and he immediately realizes what he is doing.

Keith was raised in the Ozarks, born in a farmhouse in the back country, down a rocky lane and across from a cow field lined with wild blackberries, a steep hill rising straight from the back porch. As a boy he walked the woods, his feet naturally finding the easy way among all the stones, limbs, and golf ball sized black walnut hulls and acorns as he gazed upward into the trees. If he doesn't actively think about what he is doing, his feet still do that from long ingrained habit. He's always embarrassed and aggravated with himself when he realizes what he's done to me, and he appreciates the nudges when I find myself knee high in briars.

Life is a little like that. Most of us live everyday muddling through as best we can, oblivious to anything but our own cares, our own needs, trying to make things run as smoothly as possible. What makes "a bad day" for us? When things *don't* go smoothly—a malfunctioning coffee pot, a stubborn zipper, a flat tire on the way to work, a traffic jam that makes us late when we had left in plenty of time, a spouse or toddler who had the ill grace to wake up in as foul a temper as we did.

It takes active thought to control your selfish impulses and consider others. It takes effort to accomplish the difficult—self-control, self-improvement, compassion for people who, like us, don't deserve it. But that's exactly what our Lord expects of us. This is exactly the example he left us.

Even under a weight of responsibility none of us can imagine, he gave his disciples his careful attention and encouragement. Even in tension-filled situations he showed compassion to both the sick and the sinner. Even in tremendous pain and weakness, he remembered his mother and forgave the pawns of a murderous mob.

If Jesus had looked for the smooth way, none of us would ever have hope of one. But if all we look for now is the smooth way, we may as well enjoy it while we can. It's the only smooth way we will ever have.

> *Enter in by the narrow gate: for wide is the gate, and broad is the way, that leads to destruction, and many are they that enter in thereby. For narrow is the gate, and straitened the way, that leads unto life, and few are they that find it.*

> Matthew 7.13–14

13. A Trail of Feathers

When we first moved here, we were surrounded by twenty acres of woods on each side. We sat at the table and watched deer grazing at the edge of the woods while we ate breakfast. Our garden was pilfered by coons and possums that could ruin two dozen melons and decimate a forty foot row of corn overnight. We shot rattlesnakes and moccasins, and shooed armadillos out of the yard. At night we listened not only to whippoorwills singing and owls hooting, but also to bobcats screaming deep in the woods.

Then one morning I walked out to the chicken pen to gather eggs. I stepped inside warily because the rooster had a habit of declaring his territory with an assault on whoever came through the gate, and as I watched for him over my shoulder, I realized that my subconscious count of the hens was off by one or two. So I scattered the feed and carefully counted them when they came running to eat—one, two, three, four...nine, ten, eleven. One was missing.

I scoured the pen. No chickens hiding behind the coop or under a scrubby bush. I checked the old tub we used to water them just to make sure one had not fallen in, as had happened before. Nothing quite like finding a drowned chicken first thing in the morning, but no chicken in the tub. Then I left the pen and searched around it. On the far side lay a trail of feathers leading off to the woods, but Keith was away on business and there wasn't much I could do. The next morning I counted only ten chickens and found yet another trail.

We were fairly sure what was going on. So when he got back home that day, he parked the truck up by the house, pointed toward the chicken pen, and that night when the dogs started barking, he stepped outside in the dark, shotgun in hand, and flipped on the headlights. Nothing. Every night for a week, he was out with the first bark, and every night he saw nothing. But he never stopped going out to look. At least the noise and lights were saving the chickens we still had.

Then one night, after over a week of losing sleep and expecting once again to find nothing, there it was—a bobcat standing outside the pen, seventy-five feet across the field. Keith is a very good shot, even by distant headlight.

I still think of that trail of feathers sometimes and shiver. I couldn't help hoping the hen was already dead when she was dragged off, that she wasn't squawking in fear and pain in the mouth of a hungry predator.

Sometimes it happens to the people of God. We usually think in terms of sheep and wolves, and the scriptures talk in many places of those sheep being "snatched" and "scattered." It isn't hard to imagine a trail of fleece and blood instead of feathers.

I think we need to imagine that scene more often and make it real in our minds, just as real as that trail of feathers was to me. Losing a soul is not some trivial matter. It is frightening; it is painful; it is bloody; it's something worth losing a little sleep over. If we thought of it that way, maybe we would work harder to save a brother who is on the edge, maybe we would be more careful ourselves and not walk so close to the fence, flirting with the wolf on the other side.

Look around you today and do a count. How many souls have been lost in the past year alone? Has anyone bothered to set up a trap for the wolf? Has anyone even acknowledged his existence? Clipped chickens, even as dumb as they are, do not fly over a six foot fence, but a bobcat can climb it in a flash and snatch the unwary in his jaws. Be on the lookout today.

I am the good shepherd. The good shepherd lays down his life for the sheep. He who is a hired hand and not a shepherd, who does not own the sheep, sees the wolf coming and leaves the sheep and flees, and the wolf snatches them and scatters them. He flees because he is a hired hand and cares nothing for the sheep. I am the good shepherd. I know my own and my own know me, just as the Father knows me and I know the Father; and I lay down my life for the sheep.

John 10.11–15

14. Home Canning

"Whew!" I always say when it's over for another year. Some of it is in the freezer—blueberries, strawberries, tomato sauce, corn, pole beans, white acre peas, blackeyes, and limas—but quite a bit sits on the shelves of the back pantry in those clear sturdy Mason jars: two kinds of cucumber pickles, squash pickles, okra pickles, pickled banana peppers, pickled jalapenos, tomatoes, salsa, tomato jam, muscadine juice, and muscadine jelly.

The first time I ever canned I was scared to death. First, the pressure canner scared me. I had heard too many stories of blown up pots and collard greens on the ceiling like the hanging Gardens of Babylon, but once I had used it a few times without incident, and really understood how it worked, that fear left me. I still follow the rules though, or it *will* blow up. No amount of sincerity on my part will keep that from happening if I let the pressure get too high.

I also follow the sterilization rules and the rules about how much pressure for how long and how much acidity is required for steam canning. Botulism, a food poisoning caused by foods that have been improperly canned, is a particularly dangerous disease. Symptoms include severe abdominal pain, vomiting, blurred vision, muscle weakness and eventual paralysis. You'd better believe I carefully follow all the rules for home canning. I give away a lot of my pickles and jams. Not only do I not want botulism, I certainly don't want to give it to anyone else either.

Some folks chafe at rules. Maybe that's why they don't follow God's rules. They want to take the Bible and pick and choose what suits them. "Authority?" they scoff. "Overrated and totally unnecessary." Authority does matter and a lot of people in the Bible found out the hard way. "Whatever you do in word or in deed, do all in the name of [by the authority of] the Lord Jesus" (Col 3.17). You might pay special attention to the context of that verse too.

God's people were warned over and over to follow His rules, to, in fact, *be careful* to follow His rules (Deut 5.1). I counted 31 times in the Pentateuch alone. Not following those rules resulted in death for many and captivity for others. When Ezra and Nehemiah brought the remnant back to Jerusalem, once again they were warned, at least five times in those two short books. Maybe suffering the consequences of doing otherwise made the need for so much repetition a little less.

David had a way of looking at God's rules that we need to consider. "For I have kept the ways of the Lord, and have not wickedly departed from my God. For all his rules were before me, and from his statutes I did not turn aside" (2 Sam 22.22–23). Many of David's psalms talk about God's rules, but the Psalm 119 mentions them 17 times. David calls those rules good, helpful, comforting, righteous, praiseworthy, enduring, hope-inducing, true, and life-giving. How can anyone chafe at something so wonderful?

People simply don't want rules, especially with God. God is supposed to be loving and kind and accept me as I am. No. God knows that the way we are will only bring death. We must follow the rules in order to live. We must *love* the rules every bit as much as David did. "I will praise you with an upright heart when I learn your righteous rules…My soul is consumed with longing for your rules at all times…When I think of your rules from of old, I take comfort, O Lord…Great is your mercy O Lord, give me life according to your rules" (119.7, 20, 52, 156).

I get out my canning guide and faithfully follow the rules every summer. I never just guess at it; I never say, "That's close enough." I know if I don't follow those rules someone could die, maybe me or one of my good friends or one of my precious children or grandchildren. I bet there is something in your life with rules just as important that you follow faithfully. Why then, are we so careless with the most important rules we have ever been given?

> *For this is the love of God, that we keep his commandments. And his commandments are not burdensome.*

1 John 5.3

15. *Shudder*

We had no land when we first moved to the country and were forced to rent a house in the small hamlet nearby. We were only in that big old frame house for five months, but I will never forget it. Uneven flooring, tall drafty ceilings, and, when we moved in, no heat and no running water. It was January 1st. We sat around the table in hats and coats eating oatmeal or soup for every meal, and hauling water in buckets. Eventually the truck company next door let us hook our garden hose to their well spigot. We pulled the hose through an inch wide gap under the kitchen window and ran it into the sink beneath, which at least made the haul shorter.

After about a week the well man came out and fixed the pump, and the gas man filled the tank. Still it wasn't warm. Room-sized gas space heaters in the bathroom, kitchen, and living room did little to mollify the effects of fifteen foot ceilings and cracks between the planks in the floor through which we could see the ground three feet beneath. It was the coldest winter I remember in this area—but maybe it was just that house.

When early spring rolled around I remember standing on the back stone steps in the sun—probably for the warmth. Keith was on his haunches petting the dog, a black and brown mixed breed we had picked up at the pound a year earlier and named Ezekiel. The boys were standing next to him listening, probably to some daddy advice. They were 4 and 2, oblivious to our living conditions, and perfectly happy.

Suddenly the breeze picked up and over the house something floated down out of the sky and landed across Keith's shoulders, hanging down on each side of his chest. It was a snakeskin. When we figured out what it was, he couldn't get it off fast enough. It must have been four feet long, with perfect scale imprints all along its length. It creeped me out, as the kids say these days. I still shudder when I think of it. Maybe *that's* why I still remember that house so well.

I remembered that house and that event again recently when we passed a fifty gallon drum by the woodpile and there lying across it was another perfect snakeskin, three feet long, hanging over each side of the barrel. They still give me the creeps when I see them, or the heebie jeebs, or whatever you choose to call that horrible feeling that runs down your spine, makes you shiver to your shoes and your hair stand on end. Maybe it's because I know that somewhere nearby there is a real snake. I can't pretend there aren't any out there simply because I haven't seen one lately.

I'm sure you could make of list of things that give you that feeling. What worries me is that nowhere on anyone's list is the three letter word "sin." It ought to give us the creeps to be around it, to see its effects on the world, people fulfilling their every lust, their hearts full of hate and envy and covetousness, lying as easily as they breathe. It ought to make us shiver to hear the Lord's name taken in vain from nearly every mouth, even children, or the coarse, crude, vulgar language that passes for conversation—and entertainment!—these days. Why? Because you can be positive the Devil is somewhere nearby. He's just waiting to drop out of nowhere and drape his arm around your shoulder. Before you know it, you will be dressing like everyone else, talking like everyone else, and acting like everyone else. In short, you will *be* like everyone else, walking around swathed in snakeskin, hugging it to yourself instead of ripping it off in disgust.

Don't think it can't happen to you, especially if sin doesn't give you the creeps to begin with.

> *The fear of the LORD is hatred of evil. Pride and arrogance and the way of evil and perverted speech I hate.... Seek good, and not evil, that you may live; and so the LORD, the God of hosts, will be with you, as you have said. Hate evil, and love good, and establish justice in the gate; it may be that the LORD, the God of hosts, will be gracious to the remnant of Joseph.... Let love be genuine. Abhor what is evil; hold fast to what is good.*
>
> Proverbs 8.13; Amos 5.14–15; Romans 12.9

16. Power Outage

In the country the power can go out for no apparent reason. You expect it in a storm. Limbs break and fall on power lines. Ground becomes saturated with rain and the trees uproot themselves and fall over, taking the lines underneath with them. Lightning strikes sub-stations and transformers. All of that is understandable. What is not is an outage on a calm, sunny day, something that happens far more often in the country than in town.

When you are not expecting an outage, it can cause problems. I once put a sour cream pound cake in the oven only to have the power go out twenty minutes later. (Yes, the sun was shining brightly.) I needed another 40–60 minutes of 325 degree heat. I was afraid to take the cake out, but unsure how the residual heat would affect the cooking time, nor how the reheat time would affect it when the power came back on.

I decided to leave it in the oven, thinking that it was less likely to fall from that than from suddenly moving it from the oven heat to room temperature when it wasn't even half-cooked. Two hours later, the lights came on and the oven began reheating itself. I compromised on the time and with the aid of a toothpick was able to find the moment when the cake was done but not over done. It was a little more compact than usual, but it didn't fall, and it tasted fine.

When you live in the land of unexpected outages, you really appreciate the consistency of God's power. Ephesians 1.19

tells us it is immeasurable, which means it cannot be contained and is therefore infinite. Romans 1.20 simply mentions "the eternal power" of God. Whenever we need it, it is there for the asking and nothing can deplete it. Every time I hear someone say, "There are so many others with bigger problems, I hate to bother God with mine," I wonder if they really understand the "eternal" power of God.

God's power guards us (1 Pet 1.5); it strengthens us (Eph 6.10; Col 1.11); it preserves us (Psa 79.11); it supports us in our suffering (2 Tim 1.8); it redeems us (Neh 1.10). Paul prayed that the Ephesian brethren would know that power, the same power that raised Christ from the dead (1.19–20) and the same power that can answer any request we might possibly think of (3.20). And, he says, that same power works within us as well.

When the storms of life rage around you, you will not have to worry about the power going out. In fact, that power will be stronger the more you need it. Paradoxically, we are never stronger than when we need God the most because we are letting Him take care of things. Counting on yourself is the weakest you will ever be, and that usually happens on the sunny days, the days when life is easy. On stormy days, the days when we finally give up and lay it all before God, the power at our disposal is awesome.

The Light never goes out, or even dims in a brownout, when run by the power of God.

Ascribe power to God, whose majesty is over Israel, and whose power is in the skies. Awesome is God from his sanctuary; the God of Israel—he is the one who gives power and strength to his people. Blessed be God!

Psalm 68.34–35

17. The Wood Stove

I live in Florida but up here in North Florida we still have a little bit of winter. Usually on cold nights, we fill up the wood-stove, which burns out by morning and we don't need any more till the next night, or maybe not for a few nights, depending upon the vagaries of cold fronts. Sometimes, though, I have had to keep that fire burning all day, adding a log or two every couple of hours. You see, if you let it burn down too far, it goes out. Even adding wood will do you no good if the coals are no longer glowing.

Sometimes we let our souls go out. Instead of stoking the fire, adding fuel as needed, we seem to think we can start it up at will and as needed, with just a single match I suppose. Try holding a match to a log—a real log, not a manufactured pressed log with some sort of lighter fluid soaked into it. You will find that you cannot even get it to smoke before the match dies. Starting a fire anew takes a whole lot more effort than just keeping the old one going.

God has a plan that keeps the fire going. He has made us a spiritual family. He commands us to assemble on a weekly basis. He has given us a regular memorial feast to partake of. He has given us his Word to read any time we want to. He will listen to us any time of the day. And perhaps, knowing how he has made us, that is why those songs he has given us keep going round in our heads all week—words at the ready to help us overcome and to remind us who we are. All of these things will keep the fire from dying. Just as those people who actually saw and heard Jesus on a daily basis said, "Did not our hearts burn within us while he talked to us on the road, while he opened to us the Scriptures?" Luke 24.32, his voice can come to us through the Word, through the teaching in our assemblies, and through the brothers and sisters he has given us.

Once a month attendance won't keep the fire burning. Seeing our spiritual family only at the meetinghouse will not stoke the fires of brotherly love. Picking up our Bibles only when we dust the coffee table won't blow on the embers enough to keep them glowing. Sooner or later my heart will grow cold, and no one will be able to light a big enough match to get it warm again.

Our God is a consuming fire, and he expects that to be exactly what happens to us—for us to become consumed with him and his word and his purpose. Nothing else should matter as much.

Take a moment today to open up that woodstove of a heart and see how the fire looks. Throw in another log before the fire goes out.

My heart became hot within me. As I mused, the fire burned; then I spoke with my tongue: "O LORD, make me know my end and what is the measure of my days; let me know how fleeting I am! Behold, you have made my days a few handbreadths, and my lifetime is as nothing before you. Surely all mankind stands as a mere breath! Selah. Surely a man goes about as a shadow! Surely for nothing they are in turmoil; man heaps up wealth and does not know who will gather! And now, O LORD, for what do I wait? My hope is in you.

Psalm 39.3–7

18. Slaughter

While the boys were still at home, we raised pigs and chickens. The chickens we kept mainly for their eggs, but when one stopped producing well, it was time for chicken and dumplings. The pigs were meant for meat from the time they were piglets. We named the males Hamlet and the females Baconette to remind us. You don't want to get close to an animal destined for the dining table, but then adult pigs are so disgusting there isn't much danger of that anyway.

Slaughtering chickens is not quite as traumatic as slaughtering pigs. They are birds instead of mammals, and they are small and don't bleed as much. We never shielded the boys from these things. They needed to understand where our food came from. I think there are some city people who must think meat is left in the meat markets in the night by elves the way they go on about the cruelty of ranchers and hunters. When you understand where it comes from, you respect the animals and appreciate them much more than you would otherwise. Both of our boys love animals and treat them kindly but they are strong-minded enough to understand necessity too.

Lucas learned that respect in a more difficult way than we intended. When it was time to put down a pig, Keith got up early, killed the animal and bled him as quickly as possible, and then loaded it on the trailer for the trip to the butcher. Three hundred pounds of dead weight meant he needed help.

When Lucas was finally big enough to actually help load, he went out with his dad to the pigpen and soberly watched the proceedings. Mindful of the effect it might have on him, Keith quickly poured sand on the blood. Then he backed the truck and trailer over to the pigpen gate and Lucas crawled in on the other side to help load the pig—stepping right into that camouflaged pool of blood. It rose around his ankles, warm and sticky. After his dad left for the butcher, he came in to wash his feet, a little green around the gills and pale as a ghost. He really understood the sacrifice that pig had made to feed our family.

I suppose that is why the Lord intended for us to have a weekly reminder of the sacrifice he made for us, in all its gore. Too often in asking forgiveness we are like the city folks buying meat at the grocery store, not really understanding all that made that purchase possible. We need to come to grips with the fact that our actions caused a death, a particularly horrible death. Even more than that, we are the reason for it yet again every time we sin. The way we treat our failings as something to laugh about or shrug off as trivial, we probably need to stand beneath that cross and step ankle deep in the still warm blood of Jesus to jolt us back into reality.

Sin is just as horrible as slaughter. In fact, it caused a slaughter which will prevent another one, but not if we don't have enough appreciation for it to make ourselves do better.

> *He was wounded for our transgressions, he was bruised for our iniquities; the chastisement of our peace was upon him; and with his stripes we are healed. All we like sheep have gone astray; we have turned every one to his own way; and Jehovah has laid on him the iniquity of us all. He was oppressed, yet when he was afflicted he opened not his mouth; as a lamb that is led to the slaughter, and as a sheep that before its shearers is dumb, so he opened not his mouth. ... Yet it pleased Jehovah to bruise him;*

he has put him to grief: when you shall make his soul an offering for sin, he shall see his seed, he shall prolong his days, and the pleasure of Jehovah shall prosper in his hand.

Isaiah 53.5–7, 10

19. Running Water

I wonder if it means as much to us. I wonder if it would have even gotten our attention. We take so much for granted, so many things people have not always had access to, things they would marvel at were they alive today.

Noon on a hot, dusty day saw a thirsty man sitting by a well after a long walk. A woman trudged up, not during the normal hours of drawing water; a woman, we would later discover, who was on the fringes of her society, a society that was on the fringes itself, especially to people like this man, who sat where she had hoped to find no one. To her utter amazement, he asked her for a drink. It was not just that she was from a hated caste, but she was a woman, and men seldom talked to women in public, especially not one with her background. And not only that, but he offered her something wonderful—she would never have to come draw water from this well again. She was so excited she ran to tell the others in the town, even the ones who before would not speak to her because of her questionable morals.

He stayed for two days, teaching about this miraculous water, water they eventually realized was not wet or even real, as the world counts reality, but far more real in the dawning light of a spiritual kingdom that would accept them all, not just those other people who hated them. Soon, everyone would have this living water available, and no one in that kingdom would be considered "second class."

I wonder if Jesus would have gotten my attention with this talk? I don't have to draw water from a well in the heat of the day—enough water to clean, bathe, cook, and stay alive. But one day, 30 years ago, that little story meant a whole lot more to me than it ever had before.

We came home from a trip to discover that our well had collapsed. We did not have the several hundred dollars it would have cost at the time to fix it. Keith had to dig a new well himself. For a month, every night after he finished the studying and home classes he conducted as a preacher, he worked on that well, even in the cold January rain, even running a fever.

A farmer neighbor filled and carted a five hundred gallon tank outside our door. That tank had held things not good for human consumption, so we used that water to carry in five gallon buckets for flushes, and pressure canners full for bathing. Every morning I went to another neighbor's house to fill up gallon jugs for the water we used to brush teeth, make tea and coffee, and wash dishes. The boys were 5 and 3, way too little to help cart water. I learned the value of carrying a bucket in each hand—balance was everything if you wanted to slosh as little as possible all over your carpets.

We learned to conserve water without even thinking about it—no more water running in the lavatory while brushing teeth, shaving, or putting in contact lenses! Suddenly, carrying water was a time-consuming, back-breaking job. Modern homes are simply not geared to anything but *running* water. It would have been much simpler to have had an outhouse in the backyard, and a pump handle in the kitchen. The amount of water that needed hauling would have been cut in half.

And after a month of that, I understood what this woman must have thought, what a luxury the concept must have seemed to her hot, weary body. Do we feel that way about "living water?" Is salvation such a luxury that we marvel at it and run to tell others? Or do we take it for granted like running water in our kitchens and bathrooms? I would not wish the month we endured on anyone else, but you know what? I think it was good for all of us.

> *Therefore with joy shall we draw water out of the wells of salvation. And in that day shall you say, Give thanks unto Jehovah, call upon his name, declare his doings among the peoples, make mention that his name is exalted.*

Isaiah 12.3–4

20. An Armload of Wood

We heat with wood. A thirty-two-year-old Ashley wood stove sits in the heart of our home—the kitchen and family room area. Our boys grew up watching their father labor with a chainsaw, axe, and splitting maul, eventually helping him load the eighteen inch lengths of wood into the pickup bed and then onto the wood racks. Every time a friend or neighbor lost a tree or several large limbs fell, the phone rang, and the three of them set off for a Saturday's worth of work that kept us warm for a few days and the heating bill down where we could pay it.

At first those small boys could only carry one log at a time, and a small one at that. Wood is heavy if still unseasoned, and always rough and unwieldy. By the time they were 10, an armful numbered two or three standard logs, even the lighter, seasoned ones. They were 16 or older before they could come close to their father's armload of over half a dozen logs, and grown men before they could match him log for log. Even that is a small amount of wood. In a damped woodstove, it might last half the night, but on an open fire barely an hour.

So I laugh when I see pictures of an 8–10 year old Isaac carrying four or five "sticks" up Mt. Moriah behind his father Abraham. To carry the amount of wood necessary to burn a very wet animal sacrifice, Isaac had to have been grown, or nearly so, not less than 16 or 17, and probably older and more filled out. In fact, in the very next chapter, Genesis 23, Isaac is 37 years old. In chapter 21, his weaning, he is somewhere between 3 and 8, probably the older end, so all we can say for certain is he is between 3 and 37 at the time of his offering. Our experience with wood carrying tells me that he was far older than most people envision.

Do you realize what that means? This may well have been a test of Abraham's faith, but it also shows that Isaac's faith was not far behind his father's. He could easily have over-powered his father, a man probably two decades north of 100, and gotten away. He, too, trusted that God would provide, even as he lay himself down on that altar and watched his father raise his hand.

How did he know? Because he watched God provide every-day of his life. He saw his father's relationship with God, heard his prayers and watched his offerings, witnessed the decisions he made every day based solely on the belief in God's promises, and his absolute obedience even when it hurt, like sending his brother Ishmael away (Gen 21.12–14). Isaac did not know a time when his family did not trust God, so he did too. "God will provide" made perfect sense to him.

When that young *man* carried that hefty load of wood up that mountain, he went with a purpose, based upon the example of his father's faith and his Father's faithfulness. Would your children be willing to carry that wood?

> *The living, the living, he thanks you, as I do this day; the father makes known to the children your faithfulness.*
>
> Isaiah 38.19

21. The Burn Barrel

We live in a rural county. We have no garbage pickup. Instead we have dumpsites at several places with recycling bins and a dumpster for household garbage. We have to haul our own trash. Ask yourself how much trash and garbage your family generates in a day. How many garbage cans do you have outside and how many times can you empty the trash indoors before your outside can is full? Now, how often would you like to drive several miles to dump your trash, and how many of those big trash cans will fit in your car? You now know one reason most of the folks out here have a pickup truck!

But this also explains the burn barrel. We keep two receptacles in the house—one for wet garbage and one for burnable trash. The more we can burn, the less often we have to cart garbage cans down the highway. We put everything we possibly can in that box of trash—junk mail, out-of-date documents, bills, and receipts, cardboard boxes, empty plastic containers and lids, plastic bottles and bags, old rags, irreparable clothes—everything that will burn, or melt and then burn. Don't talk to me about recycling. We recycle in several other ways, and this practice saves gas.

But let me ask you this. Would you ever put anything important in a burn barrel? Of course not. Do you know what God thinks of this world? He has his own burn barrel, and this world is what He plans to throw in it.

We need to remember that. Too often we become enamored of the very things God will ultimately destroy. Some of our favorite things in life are sitting in God's burn barrel. Even when we think we have our priorities straight, we often do not.

I remember telling my little boys that one day we would take a month long camping trip out west. We would show them all those beautiful national parks they had only heard about. They could look across the Grand Canyon, watch Old Faithful erupt, and stand in a place where the mountains rose peak after peak after peak with no signs of modern man—no power lines, no sounds of traffic, not even a tangled skein of contrail in the perfect blue sky—a place where a thousand years before some native had stood and enjoyed the same view. It never happened. We never had the money or the time. They are grown now and can understand the pressures of life, making a living, paying the bills, meeting one's responsibilities to others, but I have always felt bad about missing that trip. We managed one or two other things while they were still at home, but never that one.

But remember this, no matter how good a plan it was, how good the values we were trying to instill with an appreciation of God as the Creator of all that majestic beauty, God Himself doesn't think that much of it. It's temporary. He plans to destroy it all. The things God meant for me to teach those boys were things I could teach any time, any place, no matter how much money we did or didn't have.

The Bible is full of people who did not have the right priorities—Esau for one, who sold a birthright for one meal. The Hebrew writer calls him "profane" (Heb 12.16). Paul talks about having a "mind of the spirit" rather than a "mind of the flesh" (Rom 8.6). And why? Because Jesus' kingdom is "not of this world" (John 18.36). It is "not meat and drink" (Rom 14.17). So many things we allow ourselves to become upset about simply do not matter. Traffic jams? Noisy neighbors? Pet peeves? Even the trials of life—precisely because it is *this* life we are becoming distracted with.

"For many walk, of whom I told you often, and now tell you even weeping, that they are the enemies of the cross of Christ: whose end is perdition, whose god is their belly, and whose glory is in their shame, *who mind earthly things*. For our citizenship is in heaven; whence also we wait for a Savior, the Lord Jesus Christ" (Phil 3.18–20). Yes, Paul says that when I let things of this life upset me to the point of distraction that my "god is my belly." I am not supposed to be minding those earthly things.

So today, think about God's burn barrel. He has a place for the things He plans to destroy, just like I do, one that gets too full too fast. God's burn barrel holds things like wealth, possessions, awards, careers, opinions, irritations, Jimmy Choo shoes, stock portfolios, time shares on the beach, cabins in the mountains, camping trips out west—even this earthly tabernacle that so many try to keep looking young. They all go in the barrel at the end of the Day. And God will light the fire Himself.

> But the day of the Lord will come like a thief, and then the heavens will pass away with a roar, and the heavenly bodies will be burned up and dissolved, and the earth and the works that are done on it will be exposed…Since all these things are thus to be dissolved, what sort of people ought you to be in lives of holiness and godliness, waiting for and hastening the coming of the day of God, because of which the heavens will be set on fire and dissolved, and the heavenly bodies will melt as they burn! But according to his promise we are waiting for new heavens and a new earth in which righteousness dwells. Therefore, beloved, since you are waiting for these, be diligent to be found by him without spot or blemish, and at peace.
>
> 2 Peter 3.10–14

22. One Fence Post at a Time

I grew up reading and playing the piano instead of playing outside where it was dangerous to someone who couldn't see well. As a result, I was about as physically un-fit as anyone could possibly be. Even after a genius of a doctor fitted my strangely shaped eyeballs with contact lenses more or less successfully in my mid-teens and I could finally see what lay in front of my feet, I had grown accustomed to sedentary activities and preferred them.

Then I had babies, gained thirty pounds and could hardly walk across the house—which is not exactly large—without gasping for air. I decided it was time to change things. Keith had jogged since I had known him. My closest friend, who lived just across the cornfield from me, also jogged. Surely I could do this, too. But I did not want to be embarrassed by how I looked doing it or by failure if indeed I couldn't.

We lived well off the highway, surrounded by woods and fields, including a small hay field and larger cow pasture. Neither of those could be seen from either the highway or the neighbors' homes. So I drove around the fields and measured them with the odometer. The hayfield perimeter measured a quarter mile and the pasture three-quarters. Now I could keep track of my progress.

Nathan was four, so that first day I set him on a hay wagon in the middle of the hayfield and jogged the quarter mile around. When I finished I thought I might pass out, or die, or both. The next morning I could hardly get out of bed, but I did and after Keith left for the meetinghouse I jogged again, but this time I went all the way around, plus one fencepost further. Once again I survived. The next day I went two fence posts past one lap, and the next day three.

The hayfield was a rectangle and I was adding my fence posts on a long side. When I finally reached the end of that side, I added the whole short side at once making one and a half laps. The day after that I added half the other long side, then the other half and the last short side, making two whole laps. Once I could do three laps I moved to the cow pasture. One lap around the pasture plus one around the hayfield and I had completed a whole mile. I could hardly believe it.

I made that progress in one month and lost ten pounds without even trying. Within six months I was jogging on the highway, a five mile circuit six days a week. I had lost thirty pounds. I was never fast. The best I ever did was the tortoise-like pace of 5 miles in 47 minutes, but it wasn't the 47 minutes that got me back to my front door that day, it was the fact that I kept going.

Sometimes we expect too much of ourselves. I have known new Christians who expected their lives to change instantly the moment they came up out of the water. They thought sinful attitudes would suddenly morph into godly ones and temptation would be a thing of the past. Once the adrenaline rush wore off and life became routine, their lack of speedy progress discouraged them. No one would expect a person such as I was to run five miles the first time she ever tried, but for some reason we expect that in our spiritual progress. We do have a lot of powerful help, but powerful doesn't mean "miraculous."

We seem to expect it of others too. If a person has a failing as a young man, it will be held against him forever. The fact that he improves is seldom noticed, but let him slip one time, even if it has been ten years, and suddenly everyone is saying, "There he goes *again*." Many of my brethren would never have allowed Peter to reach the eldership for exactly that reason. Peter's impetuosity was a problem for him, as was fear of what others thought, even after Pentecost (Gal 2), but he did improve, and those people noticed instead of saying "again," or he would never have been an elder.

Do you think others didn't have problems after their conversion? Look at the admonitions in Romans 14 and 1 Corinthians 8. They were still suffering from a background of idolatry. They couldn't eat that meat without "eating as a thing sacrificed to an idol" (8.7). That problem did not disappear overnight.

Unless we are willing to say that we have reached perfection, none of us believes that it's how fast we progress that matters. We all believe that it's the improvement that God judges. Some of us have gone farther than others, but if we have stopped and are leaning on the fence, perfectly content with where we are, God will not be pleased with us. God rewards only the one who is progressing, even if it's just one fencepost at a time.

> *Brethren, I count not myself yet to have laid hold: but one thing I do, forgetting the things which are behind, and stretching forward to the things which are before, I press on toward the goal unto the prize of the high calling of God in Christ Jesus.*
>
> Philippians 3.13–14

23. A Hole in the Watering Can

I went out to water my flowers early one morning, grabbed up the two gallon watering can and headed for the spigot. The temperature had already risen to the upper 70s, and the humidity had beaten that number by at least twenty. It dripped off the live oaks, bonking on the metal carport roof as loud as pebbles would have, but I knew that soon the plants would fold their leaves against the heat in a bid to keep as much moisture in them as possible. A morning drink was a necessity for them to survive the coming afternoon.

I picked up the filled can and began the long trudge to the flower bed. What was that? Water was running down the leg that bumped the can as I walked, so I lifted the can and examined it. A steady stream of water poured out a tiny hole not quite halfway up its side.

After a moment's thought, I picked up the pace and made it to the bed in time to pour most of the water on the flowers. Ordinarily after watering, I keep a full can next to the bed to fill the small bird bath next to it as needed, but that can would no longer hold even half its normal capacity. So after the watering, I returned to the well tank and filled it only halfway and sat it by the bath. I would have to fill it twice as often now, but at least I could get a most of a gallon out of it. Better than nothing.

We are a lot like that watering can. We should be filled to the capacity that God intended, but too often we don't hold even half of it. Paul tells us we each receive a different gift according to the grace of God (Rom 12.6); Peter tells us to use that gift as a good steward of God's grace (1 Pet 4.10). Holes in the can mean we are not using those gifts as God designed, squandering His grace in the process.

Sometimes we deny the grace. "I can't do that," we say, when God has clearly put an opportunity in front of us. Have you ever given someone a gift and had them tell you that you didn't? Of course not. Everyone knows that the giver knows what he gave, yet here we are being so ridiculous as to tell God He most certainly did not give us any gifts. *God does not put opportunities in front of us that He has not given us the ability to handle. More than anyone else—even more that we ourselves— He knows what we can and cannot do.* Denying His grace is simply disobedience.

Sometimes we cheat the grace. "I'm too busy," we tell people when something comes up. Never mind that the opportunity is squarely within my wheelhouse—if I don't want to do it, being busy is the excuse of the day. In fact, sometimes we make ourselves busy with things we prefer in order to avoid more difficult spiritual obligations. It's easier to work late one night than go visit a weak brother. It's more fun to work out with a peer ("keeping my temple healthy") than learn how to study with an older Christian who wants to share his hard-earned knowledge. Shopping must be done, but it is certainly less trouble—and a lot quicker—to go shopping alone than to take an older person who is no longer able to get out on her own. And thus our busyness has kept us from filling ourselves to capacity.

Sometimes we do our best to spoil the grace by poking the hole in ourselves. God has a purpose for each one of us. I can sabotage those plans by my own selfish choices in life. Worldliness and materialism can diminish my capacity for the spiritual. Bad habits can ruin a reputation and make me less effective. Bad decisions can make me unfit for God's original plan for me. Even if I turn myself around and repent, I may never again have the same impact I would have if I had made better choices earlier in life. I may very well have drilled a hole in the can so that it will only hold half or less what God intended it to hold.

Take a good look at your watering can this morning. God knows better than you how much it can hold. Don't deny the grace; don't squander the opportunities. Don't drill a hole where one doesn't belong. Capacity is His business, not yours, and what He wants is an overflowing can.

> *Now in a great house there are not only vessels of gold and silver but also of wood and clay, some for honorable use, some for dishonorable. Therefore, if anyone cleanses himself from what is dishonorable, he will be a vessel for honorable use, set apart as holy, useful to the master of the house, ready for every good work.*
>
> 2 Timothy 2.20–21

24. Make Sure It's Dead

When I was a city girl, nearly forty years ago, I was scared to death of snakes. I still don't like them. The difference is I can tolerate a non-poisonous one on the property now, trusting they will pay their way with all the rodents they keep out of my house; and when a poisonous one comes along I don't freeze or run around in circles, screaming in hysteria—I just dispose of the thing.

You know the best way to kill a snake? Well, it may not actually be the best way, but the city girl in me thinks it's perfect—a shotgun full of number one shot. For those of you who are still city folks, that's a load for large animals, like deer. We had a rattler once when Keith was at work, and even though I kept from freezing or panicking to the point of uselessness, I still forgot to unload the larger shot and replace it with number four, a load for smaller animals. That means when I shot that snake with that huge shot, I blew it to smithereens. As I said, I was extremely satisfied.

Well—mostly satisfied. The thing kept right on writhing. Yes, I know all about their reflexes and that they thrash about after death. But that thing was flexing and re-flexing entirely too much to suit me. So I got the .22 pistol and put a few more shots in it. *Then*, I was satisfied. When I picked the thing up with the tines of the rake to throw it into the burn barrel, it hung in chunks connected only with a few strings of skin—and it didn't wiggle at all. Best looking rattlesnake I ever saw. The boys can make fun of me all they want, and laugh about it as they have for the past thirty-something years, but that snake was dead and there was no question about it.

Some of us don't make sure the snake is dead. In fact, we not only leave it writhing, we put it somewhere for safe keeping just in case it isn't dead after all. That's how we treat repentance. I know I shouldn't be indulging, so let me put it up on the shelf instead of down here on the counter top where I can see it every day. I mustn't be that obvious about it. No! Let's get it out of the house altogether! Whatever it is.

It doesn't have to be a huge sin of the flesh. It doesn't have to be a bottle of booze or a stack of pornography. Sometimes it's a gossip-fest. I know that my friend always dishes the dirt, but I still make plans to see her every week. If for some reason I must see her, then I go with no plan for how to avoid the sin, and yesiree, it pops up and, I just couldn't help it, Lord. You know how she talks—and how I listen.

Whatever it is, God expects me to kill that snake and make sure it's dead. Another one may come my way, but there is really no good reason for the same one to be making an appearance over and over. If it does, I didn't use the buckshot—I just shot a BB and missed.

Don't cuddle up to a rattlesnake. Kill the thing, and make sure it's dead.

Besides this you know the time, that the hour has come for you to wake from sleep. For salvation is nearer to us now than when we first believed. The night is far gone; the day is at hand. So then let us cast off the works of darkness and put on the armor of light. Let us walk properly as in the daytime, not in orgies and drunkenness, not in sexual immorality and sensuality, not in quarreling and jealousy. But put on the Lord Jesus Christ, and make no provision for the flesh, to gratify its desires.

Romans 13.11–14

25. The Milk Cow

A long time ago, a local farmer allowed Keith to milk his cow. The farmer furnished the cow and the feed, while Keith furnished the labor, and we split the milk. Our cut was usually a gallon a day, which was good with two boys who drank it by the quart. I also used the cream to make our own butter. There is nothing quite like a Southern pound cake made with home-made butter, homemade sour cream, and eggs fresh out of the chicken that morning. Our mashed potatoes were so creamy you might as well have troweled them onto your hips, and the homemade ice cream so rich it had flecks of butter in it.

When a dairy cow needs milking, it needs milking, period. Keith was away overnight once, not due back till late afternoon the next day. All I could think about was that poor cow. Having nursed babies, I understood her pain. Surely I could take care of this, I thought, and help both of them.

This cow was known to be a kicker. She had only recently gotten used to Keith, finally allowing him to milk her while she ate feed from the trough. I knew the drill, so I got a bucket of feed and headed for the corral. I also knew her penchant for kicking, so I put on Keith's jacket and hat before I left the house. I thought I would look and smell like him and she would never know the difference.

As I headed for the stall she saw me coming, and began a slow walk in my direction. I made my first mistake. Keith always called her with the same phrase every day, so I did too, lowering my voice as much as possible. The cow stopped and looked at me across the fence railing. For a few minutes I thought she had me, but I held up the bucket so the scent of the feed reached her on the breeze, and she started walking again.

After that I kept my mouth shut. I simply poured the feed into the trough and waited for her to put her head down. Then I reached out and started milking. Instantly her head was up again, and she looked over her shoulder at me. I stepped back, keeping a careful eye on her hind legs, ready to jump if she looked like she was even thinking about kicking.

For a long moment we stood there eying one another. Finally, she gave a snort and shake of the head. The jig was up, as they say. For all the world it looked like she was saying, "I really need this right now, so go ahead. But don't think I'm not on to you." She put her head back in the trough, and I began milking again. It was a compromise. She gave me just enough to get the pressure off her aching udder, but not enough so I would think she had not seen through my disguise. A quart later, she stepped back from the trough, and I took both the hint and the milk into the house. When Keith got home, she gladly let him finish the job.

Isaiah had a lot to say about this same point. If a cow—a dumb unreasoning animal—can know its master, why can't we so-called intelligent human beings recognize ours? If a donkey knows where to get its sustenance, why can't we figure out who we must depend upon?

Have you ever seen a cow path? Cows learn when it is time to head for the barn, and they take the shortest route every evening at the same time, following one another down the path, until it is beaten from their hooves and so obvious anyone could follow it. I look around our world every day and marvel at how many smart people don't seem to have a clue where the path is, and what's more, brag about it. Then I look at God's people and cry for all the ones who claim to be His children, but act the same way.

> *Hear, O heavens, and give ear, O earth; for Jehovah has spoken: I have nourished and brought up children, and they have rebelled against me. The ox knows his owner, and the ass his master's crib; but Israel does not know, my people do not consider.*
>
> Isaiah 1.2–3

26. The Woodpile

We started last winter with a nearly empty woodpile—not a good thing when you depend on wood heat, even in Florida. So Keith has spent several weekends cutting deadfall from friends' and neighbors' property. Since he no longer has the live-in help he had for 20 years, it has taken him far longer than ever before. Do you want to know how he stays in such good shape? Just rely on your own brawn to heat the house one winter and you will see why he can still outwork most men half his age. Once he cuts it and hauls it back to the house, he still has to split it. Even working a little every evening after he comes home from work, much remains to be done, and he hasn't even started stacking it on the racks.

So I decided to help out. I work a half hour several mornings a week, moving the wood to the first rack. Much more and I might be endangering what little health is left in my eyes due to bending over and lifting. Seasoned wood is fairly light and, in two months, a little at a time—in this case, *very* little—I have managed to safely move several stacks of wood to the first rack. It also gives me a little outdoor time with the dogs, and a little more exercise than an elliptical machine.

Yet I could have moved much more in the same amount of time if I had not had to be so careful. Real wood from real trees is not perfectly shaped and sized. It has knots, it has stubs from limbs chopped off, and it is often curved at odd angles. When I put a log on the stack, I have to carefully push on it, moving my hand sidewise to see if anything will cause it to shift. The last thing you want is for the whole pile to fall down on you when you take one log off the top. It is almost like putting together a puzzle, finding just the right piece to fit in the spot the last couple of logs made, but because it could be dangerous to be careless, you take the time to do it right.

That's the way it is when God fits us all into his church. None of us is perfect by any means. None of us will suit everyone's notion of the ideal Christian. Some of us have knots. Most of us have stubs where we cut off our past sins. Yet God expects us to fit ourselves in, to fit each other in, no matter what we think of each other.

Surely none of us has had a Saul walk into his meetinghouse to "place membership." This was a man who "laid waste the church, entering into every house, and dragging men and women … to prison" (Acts 8.3). He "both shut up many of the saints in prisons, having received authority from the chief priests, and when they were put to death… gave [his] vote against them" (Acts 26.10). He "persecuted the church of God, and made havoc of it" (Gal 1.13). Maybe you can, but I cannot say I would have easily accepted him if my family were among the tortured and dead. It would have taken a lot of faith, a lot of strength, and a lot of help from others for me to hug the new Christian and welcome him with open arms. It would have taken someone like Barnabas to get me past it. "And when he was come to Jerusalem, he assayed to join himself to the disciples: and they were all afraid of him, not believing that he was a disciple. But Barnabas took him, and brought him to the apostles, and declared unto them how he had seen the Lord in the way, and that he had spoken to him, and how at Damascus he had preached boldly in the name of Jesus" (Acts 9.26–27).

We look at those people who managed to accept a former enemy, and not only accept him, but support him and his work, and for some reason we cannot accept a man because we don't like his sense of humor? Because we think he is a little rough around the edges? We cannot accept a woman because she doesn't have our definition of "class?" Because she has an odd belief or two? God expects us to accept one another. *He* is the one who adds to the church, not we. Maybe we need to carefully fit people in, finding mentors who can help, just as Barnabas helped Saul, but that doesn't mean we just ignore new Christians because they don't suit *our* standards.

Paul told the Roman brethren, "May the God of endurance and encouragement grant you to live in such harmony with one another, in accord with Christ Jesus that together you may with one voice glorify the God and Father of our Lord Jesus Christ. Therefore welcome one another as Christ has welcomed you, for the glory of God" (Rom 15.5–7). I think it is strongly implied that if we do not welcome each other, God will not welcome us either.

God is stacking his wood pile, carefully fitting each of us into the places where we belong. We do not have a choice who our spiritual family is. We must learn to ignore things that rub us the wrong way, instead of assuming the Divine role of deciding who can and cannot be our brother. God expects us to fit together like a jigsaw puzzle, perhaps for us to even lop off a corner to make another fit. He accepted us that way, and every brother deserves that consideration from us.

I am a companion of all who fear you, and of those who keep your precepts.

Psalm 119.63

27. The Tipping Point

After six months, working 20–30 minutes at the time, I finally finished stacking that woodpile. When it became apparent that I was near the end, and I hoped "this" would be the last load, I stacked the garden cart just a little too high.

Have you seen those old Garden Way carts? A large wooden three sided box sits on two bicycle tires, with two props in front (instead of two more wheels) and a tubular handle that comes straight out from the bottom of the cart. You lift on that handle and pull or push the cart at an angle to the ground. Basically, it's one giant lever.

Since I was hoping to finish that day, I started stacking the wood into the cart from the back, behind the wheels. Instead of laying the whole first layer, which would have been so much smarter, I kept stacking the back higher and higher. Then as I turned around to grab a log for the first layer on the front end of the cart, I heard a sudden WHAM! I was almost afraid to look, but when I did saw that the cart had tipped and fallen on its back and all that carefully stacked wood had tumbled out onto the ground. Instead of balancing the weight on, behind, and in front of the wheels, I had put it all behind the wheels. What should I have expected? God doesn't ordinarily change the laws of physics when his children act in a less than intelligent manner.

We all have tipping points and we are often just as brainless about them. God warns us over and over that sin can enslave us. It isn't something we can dabble in and then step out when we're ready to. Peter says we reach a point when we "cannot cease from sin" (2 Pet 2.14). Paul says we can become "past feeling" at which point we will "give ourselves over" to unrighteousness (Eph 4.19). He also talks about people who have their "consciences branded" (1 Tim 4.2).

Slaves were branded in the first century. When, having sinned over and over, we reach the point that we have become "obedient slaves of sin" (Rom 6.16), our consciences become branded. We may think we are free, but that is part of the entrapment. Somewhere along the line we have become addicted to our sin and we cannot stop, cannot cease, have given ourselves over to this master.

And when that happens God "gives us over" as well (Rom 1.24). Whatever we want to do, He will allow, however we want to live, He will not stand in the way. "There remains no longer a sacrifice" for us (Heb 10.26).

When do we reach that tipping point? I do not know. I do know that the thought of it scares me to death. If anything will keep me righteous, maybe that is it—the idea that somewhere along the way I can reach a point where even God gives up on me. Maybe that will make me stay away from that balancing act altogether.

Does that make me yet another kind of slave? You bet—a slave of righteousness. But tipping over in that direction will bring an entirely different result.

> *Do you not know that if you present yourselves to anyone as obedient slaves, you are slaves of the one whom you obey, either of sin, which leads to death, or of obedience, which leads to righteousness? But thanks be to God, that you who were once slaves of sin have become obedient from the heart to the form of teaching to which you were committed, and, having been set free from*

sin, have become slaves of righteousness. For just as you once presented your members as slaves to impurity and to lawlessness leading to more lawlessness, so now present your members as slaves to righteousness leading to sanctification. ... But now that you have been set free from sin and have become slaves of God, the fruit you get leads to sanctification and its end, eternal life.

Romans 6.16–19, 22

28. No Lifeguard: Swim at Your Own Risk

We see that sign a lot in Florida—on beaches, at springs and lakes, and at pools. Usually, just beyond the sign, dozens of people splash around in the water, regularly going out to depths over their heads. The risk to their lives bothers them not one wit. The fun is worth it.

Every summer my boys took the risk and I whole-heartedly allowed it. We worked them hard when they were growing up, weeding and picking the garden in the heat of a Florida summer; standing in a hot kitchen working the assembly line of produce canning and freezing, mowing an acre's worth of our five with a push mower—not a walk-behind, but a *push* mower; splitting and stacking wood for the wood stove, hauling brush, raking leaves, and dumping them for mulch. After hours of hard labor and buckets of sweat, nothing thrilled them more on a hot summer afternoon than a refreshing dip in a nearby spring.

Springs, even in Florida, are cold. It is almost painful to step into one—they will literally take your breath away. I was one who gradually eased my way in to avoid the shock, but the boys wanted to "get it over with," and usually jumped off the pier, the floating dock, or the rope swing, whatever that particular spring had as a point of entry, and if I was standing too close I "got it over with" too.

All of those places were "risky." They all lacked a lifeguard, but we still splashed away an afternoon in Blue Springs, Poe Springs, and Ginnie Springs. We tubed down the Ichetucknee River from the spring head to just before the first bridge, pulling out and picnicking at the state park on tomato sandwiches and cold watermelon straight from the garden. We even swam in the Santa Fe River and O'Leno State Park while alligators sunned themselves on the opposite shore. We weren't the only ones who took the risks. Everyone did, it seemed, because we were always standing in lines.

For some reason, the risks involved in Christianity scare people much more.

In life, it might mean sharing your life preserver with someone else, someone not as generous as you. Turning the other cheek means you might very well be slapped again. Going the second mile might mean being forced to go five or ten more. Being willing to be defrauded to avoid casting aspersion on the body of Christ might mean losing money or worse, it seems, losing face.

In our Bible study, it might mean swimming in the deep waters of profound thought, opening minds that are already made up, accepting nothing without personally verifying it, and challenging our thinking—perhaps even admitting we have been wrong about something and changing. Scary indeed!

In our conversion, it means having the faith to step out of the boat in the middle of a storm, and walk wherever the Lord leads us, with or without a beloved mate, a good friend, or various members of the family.

Christians always put themselves at risk for their Lord's sake. It is not as if we were not warned. He posts the sign Himself: Swim at Your Own Risk. But there is one difference—there *is* a Lifeguard when we take the plunge, one who has already given His life to save ours. Why not enjoy the swim when we have that guarantee of safety?

> *And he said unto them, if any man would come after me, let him deny himself and take up his cross daily and follow me. For whosoever would save his life shall lose it, but whosoever shall lose his life for my sake, the same shall save it.*
>
> Luke 9.23–24

29. Pickup Trucks

Out here in the country, just about every man has a pickup truck. Most of them are several years old, caked in mud, a little rusty, and dented here and there. That's because those trucks are *used*.

We have one too. It's nearly twenty years old, usually wears a coat of dust, and sports a bed with scrapes, dings, and lines of orange rust. It has hauled wood for our heat and leaves and pine straw for mulch. It has carried loads of dirt to landscape the natural rises and dips of our property. It has toted lawn mowers and tillers to the shop for repair. It has gone on several dozen camping trips, filled to the brim of its topper with tents, sleeping bags, coolers, suitcases, firewood, and food.

Whenever we go to town, it always amuses me to see a man in a tie get out of a pickup truck, especially if that truck is clean, polished, and less than two years old. I asked such a man once why he needed his pickup. "To drive," he said. What? Isn't that what far more economical cars are for? He actually took better care of his truck than his car, polishing it to a high enough sheen to blind the driver in the next lane, and vacuuming it almost daily. Obviously, his pickup was for show. "A man ought to have a truck after all." Why? Because it makes him a man?

Before you shake your head, consider that this happens with many more things than pickup trucks. Why do you have the type of car you do? Not a car, but that particular one. I know some people who think the brand is the important part, that somehow it says something special about them. Why do you live where you do in the type of house that you have? Is it a big house because you have a big family, because you use it to house brethren passing through who need help, because you show hospitality on a regular basis? Or is it because someone of your status ought to have a house that size in that neighborhood?

I suppose the saddest thing I have seen is women who have children because "that's what women do." Their careers or busy schedules or social standing is far more important than the child, who is raised by someone else entirely, with mommy making "quality time" whenever she can spare a moment or two.

The Israelites of the Old Testament had similar problems. They wanted a king "like the countries round about them." Somehow they thought it made them a legitimate nation. Do we do similar things in the church?

Why do we have a preacher? I have heard people say we need one to look valid to the denominations around us. Why do we have a building? "Because that would make us a real church." Neither of those things is wrong to have, but our attitudes show us to be less than spiritual, not to mention less than knowledge-able, when we say such things.

Why do you have elders? "Because a church this size ought to." That may very well be, but you don't fix the problem of a church that hasn't grown enough spiritually to have qualified men by choosing men who are anything but just so you can say you have elders.

A lot of us are just silly boys who think that having a pickup truck makes them real men. Let's get to the root of the problem. What makes you a Christian, what makes a church faithful, is a whole lot like what makes you a man, and outward tokens have nothing to do with it.

"As for you, son of man, your people who talk together about you by the walls and at the doors of the houses, say to one another, each to his brother, 'Come, and hear what the word is that comes from the LORD.' *And they come to you as people come, and they sit before you as my people, and they hear what you say but they will not do it; for with lustful talk in their mouths they act; their heart is set on their gain. And behold, you are to them like one who sings lustful songs with a beautiful voice and plays well on an instrument, for they hear what you say, but they will not do it. When this comes—and come it will!—then they will know that a prophet has been among them."*

Ezekiel 33.30–33

30. Running Down to the Store

Living in the country has meant adapting. In many ways it has been good for me. The city girl found out she could learn and change, even though change is a thing I have never liked. I love routine. Now, after 32 years, it isn't change, it's just a new routine, and that helps when I have had many more changes in the past few years, and see more coming.

One of the things I learned quickly was to make sure I had everything I needed to get by for the week. A sixty to eighty mile round trip, depending upon which side of town what I need is on and how many other places I have to stop as well, doesn't happen more than once a week even if you did forget the bread or run out of milk. You learn to do without. You don't change your mind about the menu unless you already have on hand the things the preferred dish needs. When an unexpected guest arrives and you want to offer a meal, you put another potato in the pot, double the biscuit recipe, and get out another package of frozen garden corn, and if you didn't plan dessert that night, you put the home-canned jellies and jams on the table. So far, no one has complained.

I have learned to be organized. I do everything in one visit, and usually that coincides with a doctor appointment or a women's Bible class. I keep track of everything I run out of, or run low on, as the week progresses, and buy it all in the order that uses the least gas. I keep staples well stocked.

I have also learned that I don't have to have everything I think I do. The only store close to us is a tire store, about three miles down the country highway. The man has been in business for 40 years. Our children went to school with his, and somehow he has made a good living selling tires in the smallest county in Florida just outside a village that might have a population of 100 if you count the dogs. But as far as shopping, it doesn't do much for me. You can't try tires on, they don't do much for the home décor, and window shopping is the pits. So I don't "shop."

Sometimes we become slaves to our culture. We think we must wear certain things, go certain places and do things in a certain way because everyone else does. We shop and buy because everyone does, not because we need it. We go see the movies that "everyone" has seen. We buy a cell phone because "everyone" has one nowadays—"it's a necessity." We run down to the store every time we run out of something instead of carefully making a list of what we need and taking care of it in one, or at most two trips a week, wasting precious time and costing ourselves more money than we realize. *Everyone* does, we say. Maybe we should stop and think about that.

Why? First, because it never crosses our minds to be different than *everyone*. Is it sinful? Maybe not, but then why does something have to be sinful before I am willing to look at it and decide whether it is best for me and my situation? Why am I so afraid to be different? A Christian should have a mindset that is always looking at things in different ways than the rest of the world. If I decide this is the best way to live (and not sinful), then fine, but I should, at the least, *think* about it. Christians who always act without thinking will eventually do something wrong some time in the future.

Second, we are to be good stewards of everything God gives us, including time and money. If we saved a little time, could we use it in service to God? Could we offer help to someone in distress? Would we have more time for visiting the sick and studying with neighbors? If we saved those few dollars every week, could we give more to the Lord? Could we help someone in need more often? Could we be the ones who take a bag of groceries to a family in distress because that day we could buy for them instead of running to the store for yet something else we forgot?

But we aren't really talking about running down to the store here. We're talking about attitude and priorities—about doing the best we can for our Master in more than a haphazard way. Paul says we are to "purpose," or plan, our giving. I have no doubt that doing so ensures a larger donation than merely waiting till the last minute to see what's left in the bank or the wallet. The same thing will be true if we plan our prayer time, study time, and service time. Instead of running out of time for any of it, we will find ourselves making a habit of the things God expects of us.

In a parable Jesus praised the steward who was "a faithful and wise manager," who was always working, always serving, and able to get the appropriate things done at the appropriate time (Luke 12.42). Those servants, he goes on to say, are always ready for the master's return. Are we ready, serving and working as many hours a day as possible as faithful stewards, or are we so disorganized that judgment day will find us at the checkout for the fifth time in a week, just to pick up a forgotten jug of milk?

As each has received a gift, use it to serve one another, as good stewards of God's varied grace: whoever speaks, as one who speaks oracles of God; whoever serves, as one who serves by the strength that God supplies—in order that in everything God may be glorified through Jesus Christ. To him belong glory and dominion forever and ever. Amen.

1 Peter 4.10–11

31. In Hot Pursuit

I grew up in Central Florida so I am familiar with houseflies. We even had them in the winter. After every annual Thanksgiving and Christmas dinner at my grandmother's house, she pulled all the food to one end of the table, then carefully draped the other end of the tablecloth back over the bowls and platters for anyone who wanted to snack all day. That way the flies couldn't use the food as landing strips.

When Keith and I moved to the country, flies became an ordeal. Even with air conditioning, they manage to zoom in between door openings and closings, especially when, as was the case for several years, not twenty feet outside your back door lies a well-populated cow pasture.

What I was not ready for were yellow flies. I had never dealt with a fly that bites. The first time one landed for a snack, it left me with a hard, sore knot the size of a ping pong ball. Keith tells me this is not the usual case, that I must be hypersensitive, but whatever is going on here I do my best to stay away from yellow flies.

When I jogged, I always passed one place on the road where one particular yellow fly made it his business to give me grief. He buzzed my head like a crop duster, and I am sure my pace increased to near world record speeds on that hundred foot stretch of highway every day. I am also certain I looked pretty funny swinging and swatting away with both hands, but it was the only way to keep myself free of those painful welts.

I thought of that fly chasing me down the road when I read this verse: "But as for you, O man of God…pursue righteousness, godliness, faith, love, steadfastness, and godliness" (1 Tim 6.11).

Most of the time we focus on the things we are supposed to be pursuing in that passage, but did you ever wonder exactly *how* you should be pursuing them? Like a yellow fly, as it turns out.

"And falling to the ground he heard a voice saying to him, "Saul, Saul, why are you persecuting me?" And he said, "Who are you, Lord?" And he said, "I am Jesus, whom you are persecuting" (Acts 9.4–5).

I did a little research into that word "pursue" and those are the verses that popped up. "Pursue" is translated more than any other English word, more in fact, than all of the choices put together, as "persecute," just as it is in Acts 9. We are supposed to "persecute" all righteousness, godliness, faith, love, steadfastness, and meekness. What?!

Just think for a minute about how Saul went about persecuting Christians. He went from city to city. He made appointments with the authorities to get what we might think of as warrants in order to put them in prison. Then he testified against them to make his case. Many times this persecution was "to the death." Once he finished in one place, he moved to the next, and to the next, and to the next. Persecuting Christians was his *life*.

How much of our lives do we spend trying to become more righteous, more godly, more loving, and all those other things that Paul says we should *pursue*? How much time, how much effort, how much sacrifice do we give to it? Or do we instead offer excuses for poor behavior we should have mastered years ago, for sins we refuse to overcome? If we were pursuing righteousness the way Paul pursued—persecuted—Christians, if we spent our lives doing whatever was necessary to learn to love as we ought, if we "buffeted our bodies" to become more godly, if we spent the same amount of time bolstering our faith that we do soothing our egos or building our bank accounts, maybe those things wouldn't be so difficult to chase down.

When I think about being pursued by that pesky, persecuting yellow fly, I instantly understand what I *should* be doing to become a better disciple of my Lord. Come out and visit some day and I'll see if we can't arrange the same experience for you!

> *Follow after (pursue, persecute) peace with all men and holiness,* **without which no one shall see the Lord.**
>
> Hebrews 12.14

32. Ultimate Croquet

A long time ago we gave the boys a croquet set. At first they seemed a little disappointed—croquet? How boring. Then we actually started playing and they discovered strategy, like whacking your opponent completely out of bounds with one of your free shots. Now that was fun.

We have settled down to annual games during the holidays whenever we get together. It is the perfect way to let the turkey digest, and we usually wind up playing two or three times. But that time of year means a less than clear playing field on what is already a rollercoaster lawn. Our yard, you see, isn't exactly a lawn. It's an old watermelon field, and though the rows have settled somewhat after thirty years, we still have low spots, gopher holes, ant hills, and armadillo mounds. But in the fall we also have sycamore leaves the size of paper plates, pine cones, piles of Spanish moss, and cast off twigs from the windy fronts that come through every few days between October and March. You cannot keep it cleaned up if you want to do something besides yard work with your life. So when you swing your mallet, no matter how carefully you have aimed, you never really know where your ball will end up. We call it "ultimate croquet." Anyone who is used to a tabletop green lawn would be easy pickings for one of us—even me, the perennial loser.

All those "hazards" make for an interesting game of croquet, but I have learned the hard way that an interesting life is not that great. I have dug ditches in a flooding rainstorm, cowered over my children during a tornado, prayed all night during a hurricane, climbed out of a totaled car, followed an ambulance all the way to the hospital, hugged a seizing baby in my lap as we drove ninety down country roads to the doctor's office, bandaged bullet wounds, hauled drinking water and bath water for a month, signed my life away before experimental surgeries—well, you get the picture. Give me dull and routine any day.

Dull and routine is exactly what Paul told Timothy to pray for. "I exhort therefore, first of all, that supplications, prayers, intercessions, thanksgivings, be made for all men; for kings and all that are in high place; that we may lead a tranquil and quiet life in all godliness and gravity. This is good and acceptable in the sight of God our Savior; who would have all men to be saved, and come to the knowledge of the truth" (1 Tim 2.1–4).

Did you catch that? Pray that our leaders will do what is necessary for us to have a "tranquil and quiet life" so that all men can "come to a knowledge of the truth." God's ministers cannot preach the gospel in a country where everyone is in hiding or running in terror from the enemy, where you never have enough security to sit down with a man and discuss something spiritual for an hour or so, where you wonder how you will feed your family that night, let alone the next day. The *Pax Romana* was one of the reasons the gospel could spread—peace in the known world. That along with the ease of travel because every country was part of the same empire and a worldwide language made the first century "the fullness of times" predicted in the prophets.

I don't have much sympathy for people who are easily bored, who seem to think that life must always be exciting or it isn't worth living. I am here to tell you that excitement isn't all it's cracked up to be. And God gave us plenty to do during those dull, routine times. It's called serving others and spreading the Word. If you want some excitement, try that. It's even better than Ultimate Croquet.

> *Now concerning brotherly love you have no need for anyone to write to you, for you yourselves have been taught by God to love one another, for that indeed is what you are doing to all the brothers throughout Macedonia. But we urge you, brothers, to do this more and more, and to aspire to live quietly, and to mind your own affairs, and to work with your hands, as we instructed you.*
>
> 1 Thessalonians 4.9–11

33. Cell Towers

We went a long time before we finally gave in and bought a cell phone. It was an expense we did not need, and an aggravation we did not want. I am not the servant of my phone and will not allow it to have me running at its beck and call! But finally the phone companies took down most of the phone booths I had used when there was an emergency or I just needed to make some unexpected last minute arrangements. I had to have a phone for those things.

It still isn't the cure for everything. Especially where I live. While I may be one of the only people in the state of Florida to actually use her cell phone for emergencies only, when I need to use it, I really need to use it. Then it becomes more than a little aggravating to get only one or two bars or worse, the big red X— no service. Wherever that tower is, it is to the southwest, and I have spent a lot of time wandering around in my southern field trying to turn that red X into at least three bars so I will hear more than static and be less likely dropped.

Once I was meandering with such rapt attention on that tiny little screen that when I finally got my three bars and stood stock still so I wouldn't lose them, I found myself jumping around a moment later, covered in fire ants. The only place I could get reception was in an ant bed!

But cell towers do not matter when you need the Lord. Whenever His children need Him, he is just a word or a thought away. You don't even have to dial, and you certainly don't have to wander around outside in the heat or cold or rain trying to get a signal. "Draw near to God and He will draw near to you," James tells us (4.8). Indeed when I looked up the word in a concordance, I discovered that the only reason God is ever "far" from us is because we have gone far from Him (Isa 29.13; 33.13; 46.12; etc.).

The next time you pull out that little monstrosity, remind yourself how blessed you really are. You have a Father in Heaven who will answer your call no matter how many bars your spirit has left within you. He will hear you, even if you only have strength left to whisper.

> *Let us then with confidence draw near to the throne of grace,*
> *that we may receive mercy and find grace to help in time of need*
>
> Hebrews 4.16

34. A Morning Fire

After an unseasonable two weeks in the month of January that left our azaleas and blueberries blooming, the live oak leaves falling by the bushel, and the air conditioner humming away instead of the woodstove, we finally had a night in the thirties and woke February 1 to frost on the ground—and on all those blooms.

Keith rose earlier than usual to start the sprinkler on the blueberries so when the sun hit them as it climbed behind the trees in the eastern woods, the frost would be washed off and the blooms left undamaged. He also built a small fire in the fire pit beside them, pulled together from the remains of a fire we had enjoyed the night before with a cup of hot chocolate.

Ever since we moved to this plot of ground we have had a fire pit for hot dog fires and marshmallow roasts. Now with the boys gone, we still like to sit there on a cold night and talk. We sit there in the mornings too, if coals remain, and some did that day, so, thanks to a considerate husband, I had a fire to warm me along with my second cup of coffee.

The world was waking up. Wrens warbled loudly in the shrubs, in between perches on the suet cage. The hawks cried out as they flew overhead, hunting breakfast. A neighbor's cow bawled so loudly I wondered if it needed milking or was just hungry. Frosted off brown grass may be crunchy, but probably doesn't offer much nourishment.

I watched the small fire and scratched Chloe's furry head. Suddenly the wood shifted, and the whole fire lowered a bit as the wood beneath completely lost its framework and became nothing but ashes. Slowly and surely the rest began to burn and fall, and within a few minutes only a twig or two was left glimmering in the white debris beneath.

One morning recently, when we were sitting by a similar fire planning a camping trip, we suddenly realized that we could no longer plan "twenty years from now" with any reasonable expectation. I suppose it hit me first when I did the math and thought, if Keith makes it twenty more years he will have outlived all of his grandparents and his father. Twenty years will still have me five years short of my mother's current age, and nearly forty years short of one of my grandmother's. Then I realized that I take after my other grandmother more and that would give me only fourteen more years.

I am not being morose. After all, for a Christian, it means the reward is closer, but I think the day it hits you will suddenly change everything you say and do from then on. It needs to hit you sooner rather than later—life is short, a breath, a wind, a shadow, the grass, the flowers—all of these things are mentioned in scores of places in the scriptures.

We are just like that small morning fire. Only half the size of a normal campfire and built on the half burnt remains of the night before, it was gone in moments. But it still accomplished two things.

It provided some warmth in the early morning chill. The thermometer next to the house said 37 that day, but Keith said the car thermometer, which was not next to a warm wall, registered between 29 and 33 as he drove to work. In a nightgown, sweatshirt and denim jacket, I needed some warmth while I sat there. So does the world. It's up to me to provide that warmth, which translates as comfort and compassion, to everyone I meet. As Paul said, "Blessed be the God and Father of our Lord Jesus Christ, the Father of mercies and God of all comfort, who comforts us in all our affliction, so that we may be able to comfort those who are in any affliction, with the comfort with which we ourselves are comforted by God" (2 Cor 1.3–4). God gives us spiritual life so we can give comfort to others, not just for our own joy.

The morning was still dim that day, and the fire also provided me with the light to see around me. God appeared as a pillar of cloud to lead the Israelites during the day. What about travel after dark? "And the Lord went before them by day in a pillar of cloud to lead them along the way, and by night in a pillar of fire to give them light, that they might travel by day and by night" (Exod 13.21). Isn't it in the dark of trial, indecision, and despair that we need guidance most? And when do our neighbors need our help the most? God means for us to be a light, a city set on a hill, bright enough for all to see even at a distance.

And then we gradually burn down and the light and the warmth disappear. Or does it? Don't you still remember people who have helped you along the way? Don't you still recall their wise and comforting words and their kind deeds? It only looks like the fire has died, for underneath those feathery white ashes lie smoldering coals that will still warm you and give you light.

That's what God expects of this small morning fire we call our lives, and the fire that keeps on giving will be the one that springs to life again on that bright and glorious morning to come.

So teach us to number our days that we may get a heart of wisdom.

Psalm 90.12

35. Chasing Pigs

We raised pigs when the boys were growing up. A pig a year in the freezer went a long way toward making our grocery bill manageable, everything from bacon and sausage in the morning to chops and steaks on the supper table, ribs on the grill, and roasts and hams on our holiday table. The first time the butcher sent the head home in a clear plastic bag and I opened the freezer to find it staring at me nearly undid me though. After that Keith made sure to tell them to "keep the head."

We bought our pigs from a farmer when they were no more than 30 pounds. That created a problem that usually the boys and I were the only ones home to deal with. Once the pigs were over 100 pounds they could no longer root their way under the pen, but those young ones did it with regularity, especially the first week or so when they had not yet learned this was their new home and they could count on being fed. More than one morning I went out to feed them and found the pen empty, spending the remainder of my morning looking for the pig out in the woods.

One Wednesday evening when Keith had to work, the boys and I stepped outside to load us and our books into the car for the thirty mile trip to Bible study, only to see the young pig, probably 40 pounds by that time, rooting in the flower beds. We spent the next forty-five minutes chasing it. You would think three smart people, two of them young and agile and me not exactly decrepit in those earlier days, could corner a pig and herd him back to the pen. No, that pig gave chase any time any one of us got within twenty feet of him, and they are much faster than they look.

You see things in cartoons and laugh at the pratfalls exactly as the cartoonist wanted you to, knowing in your mind that such things never could happen. When you chase a pig you find out otherwise.

Once we did manage to corner the thing between a fencepost and a ditch and Lucas, who was about 12, leapt for him with his arms outstretched. Somehow that pig managed to move and Lucas landed flat on the ground on his stomach while the pig ended up trotting past all of us on his merry way, wagging his head in what looked like amusement.

Another time Lucas actually got his arms around the pig's stomach, but even an un-greased pig is a slippery creature. Nathan and I never had a chance to grab on ourselves before it was loose again and off we all ran around the property for the umpteenth time, dressed for Bible study by the way, which made the sight much more ridiculous, especially my billowing skirt.

We never did catch that pig. He simply got tired and decided to go back into the pen. I had opened the gate and as he trotted toward it, we all gratefully jogged behind him, winded and filthy and caring not a hoot that it was his idea instead of ours. Still, he had to have the last word. Instead of going through the open gate, at the last minute he ran back to where he had gotten out in the first place and slunk under the rooted out segment of the pen. Then he turned around and looked at us. "Heh, heh," I could almost hear with the look he gave us. We shut the gate, filled in the hole, loaded up the feed trough, and went inside to clean up, arriving at Bible study thirty minutes late and too exhausted and traumatized to learn much that night.

God is a promise maker. He has given us so many promises I could never list them all here. We have a habit of treating those promises like a pig on the loose, like something we can't really get a good hold of, certainly not a secure one.

I grew up in a time when it was considered wrong to say, "I know I am going to Heaven." Regardless the fact that John plainly said in his first epistle, "These things I have written that you may *know* you have eternal life" (5.13), actually saying such a thing would get you a scolding about pride, and a remonstrance like, "Let him who thinks he stands, take heed lest he fall!" We were too busy fighting false doctrine to lay hold of a hope described as "sure" in Hebrews 6.19.

That word is the same one used in Matthew 27.64–66. The priests and Pharisees implored Pilate to make Jesus' tomb "sure" so his disciples could not steal the body and claim a resurrection. He told the guards, "Make it as *sure* as you can." Do you think they would have been careless about it? Do you think there was anything at all uncertain about the seal on that tomb? Not if you understand the disciplinary habits of the Roman army. It is not quite as obvious because of the different translation choice, but the Philippian jailor was given the same order, using the same word, when Paul and Silas were put in prison: "Charging the jailor to keep them *safely* [sure]," and he was ready to kill himself when he thought they had escaped.

That is how sure our hope is—"an anchor...steadfast and *sure*." It isn't like a pig we have to chase down. It isn't going to slip through our fingers if we don't want it to. Paul told the Thessalonians that "sure" hope would comfort them (2 Thes 2.16). How comforting is it to be fretting all the time about whether or not you're going to Heaven? How reassuring is it to picture God as someone who sits up there waiting for you to slip so He can say, "Gotcha!" That is how we treat Him when we talk about our hope as anything less than certain.

I never knew what to expect when I stepped out of my door the first few weeks with a new piglet. If we hadn't needed it, I would not have put myself through the anxiety and the ordeal. Why in the world would anyone think that God wants us to feel that way about our salvation?

> *...in hope of eternal life, which God, who cannot lie, promised before times eternal.*
>
> Titus 1.2

36. Dragonflies

Keith called me outside one Saturday. I was in the middle of something important and was a little irritated. It is hard enough to do things these days when I have to lean so close, squint so hard, and put up with the resulting headaches trying to see what I am doing. Then he wants to interrupt me, and I will just have to start all over again. But I sighed, a louder one than was called for, and dutifully went outside.

The afternoon sun was waning, for which I was grateful. No matter how dim the day I have to reach for sunglasses nearly all the time now. He took me to a shaded spot on the west side of the field and pointed. Then I saw it, or them as it turned out, probably a couple hundred dragonflies darting here and there all over the place.

He felt bad for me because I could not see them all the time. In fact, I would not have known what they were had he not told me, but I think my vision of them was the best. He saw them in the shade as well, when they once again became ugly black bugs, but I only saw them as they came out of the shadows, the sun striking their wings and lighting them up like tiny golden light bulbs. Then they would disappear, but more would appear in their place, over and over, darting here and there in movements no one could possibly predict. I think my view was much more magical than his, and therefore far more delightful. We stood there watching them for several minutes. I probably could have stood their longer since I had the better view, a view he would never have because he could see so well.

No matter what we may be going through in this life, God always prepares good things for us, but we will never see them if we always stay inside ourselves, commiserating with ourselves, rewinding over and over the tape of all our troubles till we can recite them from memory to anyone who asks, and even some who don't. There is a silver lining somewhere if we just search, and in the searching who knows what treasures we might find? Besides, it will keep us too busy to complain so much.

Go out there today and look for those silver linings—or the golden dragonflies, or whatever God has specially prepared to help you through this day. You will find them, but only if you have a mind to.

> *You prepare a table before me in the presence of my enemies; you anoint my head with oil; my cup overflows. Surely goodness and mercy shall follow me **all the days of my life**, and I shall dwell in the house of the LORD forever.*
>
> Psalm 23.5–6

37. Stuck in the Mud

We live on a slope. The grade is gradual, so gradual you don't really see it until it rains one of those sub-tropical downpours for which Florida is famous. When four inches comes down in less than an hour, the property becomes a river two or three inches deep flowing downhill to the run just past the property line.

After the rain stops, the draining continues, though it slows to three or four tributaries and eventually two larger "rivers." One runs through the front yard, between the bird feeders, down around the house, across the septic drain field and off the property. Another slants southeast through the PVC pipe culvert Keith installed under the road twenty-nine years ago, down the berm on the top edge of the garden and on east.

Usually within a couple of hours most of the water has drained, but puddles still fill a few low areas, and you learn where and how to walk for the next day or two. On sandy land, the puddles dry up quickly, unless it's the second weekend in a row with a four inch toad strangler.

We learned early on to avoid those low spots for several days. We first met one of our neighbors when we asked him to pull our car out of the mud with his tractor at least three times in one week. Two months ago, for the first time in many years, he had to come down and do it again. I knew what had happened when, after two deluges in one week, I heard the truck engine roar and looked out the window to see the back tires spinning and mud flying ten feet behind them.

When you are stuck in the mud, you can't move. The wheels may rotate but all you do is dig ruts and uproot grass. The harder you press the accelerator, the deeper the ruts and the less you move. Even rocking the truck back and forth becomes impossible.

Sometimes we get stuck in the spiritual mud. It comes first with complacency. We are happy with what we know and where we are, so we sit down, clasp our hands, and contentedly lean back with our feet up on the desk. Proverbs speaks of the results of being a complacent "sluggard": "Yet a little sleep, a little slumber, a little folding of the hands to rest; so shall your poverty come as a robber, and your want as an armed man" (24.33–34). Tell me the same thing won't happen when we stop working on our spirituality.

It isn't just a matter of continuing to learn, though that is important. An older woman in one of my classes has expressed appreciation for the new things I teach her. "At my age it's hard to find something new," she said, "but you have given me that and it's wonderful." Yes, the older you are, the more difficult it *should be* to find something new to learn, so you certainly cannot sit back and fold your hands in slumber—you must work even harder to find those things and they will be even deeper than the "first principles," and require yet more thought and labor.

But it is also a matter of *progress.* I see people who haven't changed one whit in thirty years, who still fight the same battles, who still fail the same way again and again. I see people who still gossip, who still judge unfairly, who are still oversensitive and too easily offended. I see people who still have their priorities upside down instead of finally learning the higher value of the spiritual over the carnal. I see people who have come no closer to mastering self-control than when they were young and foolish—they just become too weary to go at it in their old age and that is all that has moderated their passions.

So today, check to see where you stand—or wallow. Are you stuck in the mud of worldliness and pleasure? Are you glued in the mire of wealth and possessions and financial security? Are you floundering in the quagmire of man's philosophy and false theology? Pull yourself out and start moving again. If you cannot do it alone, call a neighbor to help. That's why God put us all here together.

And when the storms come into your life again, use your head—stay away from the low spots. Find the high ground of spirituality and keep on climbing.

> *I waited patiently for Jehovah; And he inclined unto me, and heard my cry. He brought me up also out of a horrible pit, out of the miry clay; And he set my feet upon a rock, and established my goings. And he has put a new song in my mouth, even praise unto our God: Many shall see it, and fear, And shall trust in Jehovah.*
>
> Psalm 40.1–3

38. Listen Up!

I sat on the carport today since the spring breeze is still cool, and relatively dry. I was working on Proverbs with my trusty bodyguards lying at my feet, tails occasionally swishing sand across the concrete. When we first moved here, twenty-nine years ago now, it was the quietest place we had ever lived. No neighbors revving up engines of various kinds, no traffic on the highway, certainly no sirens wailing in the air. In the past two or three weeks alone, I have heard sirens three times, which is about as many times as I heard them the whole 29 years before. People are moving here to have what we have, and in the process, destroying it.

But that morning I was suddenly struck by how quiet it was—not exactly like all those years ago, but close. I sat still and really listened; half a dozen different birds sounds, chirps, tweets, squawks, caws, shrieks, and crows; wings flapping in the oaks; a June bug buzzing over our heads in the sycamore, two planes droning overhead, one a jet and the other a single-engine prop; hummingbirds humming and squeaking at the feeder; a semi roaring faintly down the highway to the west beyond the woods, hitting the speed bumps a good half mile away with a rhythmic brrrrump—brrrrump—brump, brump, brump.

Even the dogs seemed to realize how quiet things were, and they sat there with me, watching and listening. Amazing things happen when you sit quietly and just listen. A limb, evidently weakened by age and a recent wind, suddenly cracked and fell just up the driveway; a little flock of sparrows landed barely two feet off the concrete slab, hopping around on the ground as if totally unaware that a human and two dogs were nearby; a pileated woodpecker suddenly swooped down across the drive and landed on the water oak trunk and began pecking for his lunch; a lizard crept out onto the steps and puffed out his red balloon of a throat when he suddenly realized we were there; and a black and yellow swallowtail butterfly landed on an azalea limb close enough for *me* to see its spots.

I have heard that Abraham Lincoln was fond of saying, "Better to be quiet and thought a fool than to open your mouth and remove all doubt." I didn't realize that he was paraphrasing one of the proverbs: "Even a fool when he holds his peace is counted as wise; when he shuts his lips, he is esteemed as prudent" (17.28). I suppose Lincoln's version was a bit more colorful, but you get the point. Amazing things can happen when you keep your mouth shut. People may actually think you are wise!

Someone else has also noted that when your mouth is open, your ears stop working, which is just a cute way of saying that when you are talking you can't listen, and most of us need to do much more listening than talking. I would guess that the majority of times we find ourselves in hot water it is because we talked when we should have been quiet. Is there a problem in the home? At work? With a neighbor? Look back in your mind and 'listen' to what happened. Amazing things can happen when you listen. You will probably see that it all began with a word *not* fitly spoken. As James said: "Let every man be swift to hear, slow to speak and slow to wrath, for the wrath of man does not work the righteousness of God" (1.19–20).

Listening is also a good way to serve others. Don't be so quick to give advice unless it is specifically asked for. Don't be so quick to take over the conversation with how *you* handled something similar. Amazing things can happen when you listen. By having a sympathetic listener, many people can figure their way out of problems on their own, and they will be so grateful for your "help."

Ahem, men—she doesn't want you to fix it, she just wants you to listen. You will become her hero. *Truly* amazing things can happen if you just listen.

And always listen to God. Too many times we are explaining ourselves to him instead. Imagine that. This is God we are talking about and we feel the need to explain something to him? Listen instead. Maybe the problem is we don't want to hear what he has to say to us. So if you do answer back, listen to that too. You might realize your error and repent.

Amazing things can happen when you sit quietly and listen.

And Moses said, the Lord God will raise up for you a prophet like me from your brothers. You shall listen to him in whatever he tells you. And it shall be that every soul who does not listen to that prophet shall be destroyed from the people.

Acts 3.22–23

39. Fire on a Windy Day

I stepped outside a few weeks ago and saw flashing red and blue lights up the hill, far more than one vehicle's worth. Since the original neighbor died, his heirs have moved on to the property and begun tearing apart the old trailer he used as rental property. First they peeled the metal off the sides and sold it for scrap. Then they tore down the rest. Insulation and paneling littered the yard. The trailer itself was nothing more than a pile of rubbish about four feet high. That day they decided to burn it.

We have a new neighbor who lives right across from them, an older woman who raises goats and lives a quiet, orderly life. She looked outside on what was probably the windiest day of the driest month of spring to see flames just across the lime rock drive from her own house. So she called 911.

That was by far a smarter move than the other neighbors had made that day, for quite soon the fire got away from them and started spreading. Imagine that! Then, to cap off the whole ridiculous escapade—evidently some ammunition was left in the old trailer and it suddenly started going off, at least one shotgun shell and half a dozen solid bullets. Before it was over three fire trucks, an ambulance, a forestry truck, and two deputies were crowding my narrow little road. Somehow, no one was hurt.

No, my neighbors were not too bright that morning, starting a fire on a windy day in the middle of a drought and failing to make sure that all they were burning was wood and insulation.

What could we expect though? These were the offspring of a man who, on another windy day in the middle of a drought 15 years ago, gave his children some matches to play with so they would stay out of his hair. That time we were the ones almost burned out. We did lose a portion of fence when the firemen broke through it with a bulldozer while building a firebreak, but nothing else thanks to their hard work.

You know what? We often play with fire exactly the same way, with even worse consequences. Solomon says, "Do not enter the path of the wicked, and do not walk in the way of the evil. Avoid it; do not go on it; turn away from it and pass on" (Prov 4.14–15). We go where we have no business being, where temptation sits waiting to strike, and then wonder how we got into trouble.

We turn away from good advice and listen to the bad, avoid the righteous and hang around with the wicked, because we are certain we are strong and can handle the traps. "The teaching of the wise is a fountain of life, that one may turn away from the snares of death. Good sense wins favor, but the way of the treacherous is their ruin. In everything the prudent acts with knowledge, but a fool flaunts his folly" (Prov 13.14–16). I have always thought it amusing how little God cares for political correctness and tact. He calls us fools when we act like one.

God even told the Israelites not to covet the idols their neighbors had. Why? "The carved images of their gods you shall burn with fire. You shall not covet the silver or the gold that is on them or take it for yourselves, lest you be ensnared by it" (Deut 7.25). God has always pictured wealth as a snare to his people. Yet what do we always wish for? What do we think will fix all our problems? "But those who desire to be rich fall into temptation, into a snare, into many senseless and harmful desires that plunge people into ruin and destruction" (1 Tim 6.9). Let's not get on our high horses because we understand that a Christian shouldn't play around with liquor, with drugs, with gambling, or with illicit sex. For one thing, we are just as vulnerable as anyone in those areas. For another, we are just as bad when we think money is the be-all and end-all. We are playing with dynamite that could explode in our faces just as easily.

Are you playing with fire in your life? Are you too sure of yourself, so confident in your ability to overcome that you place yourself in harm's way and practically dare the Devil to come get you? Remember God's opinion of such a person. I don't want him to call me a fool on the day it matters the most.

> *Can a man carry fire next to his chest and his clothes not be burned? Or can one walk on hot coals and his feet not be scorched? The fear of the LORD is a fountain of life, that one may turn away from the snares of death.*
>
> Proverbs 6.27–28; 14.27

40. Wild Mint Among the Nettles

A few years ago Keith dug up a plant he found out in the field far from the house, surrounded by stinging nettles and poison ivy. He had thought it looked like something besides another weed. When I rubbed the leaves between my fingers and sniffed, I discovered it was spearmint. So I potted it and put it next to my herb bed, where it comes in handy every so often, and grows so bountifully I have to give it a haircut once in a while.

Imagine finding a useful herb in the middle of a patch of useless, annoying, and even dangerous weeds. I thought of that mint plant a few days ago when we studied Rahab in one of my classes. I have written about her before, and you can read that article on my blog (www.flightpaths.org: "The Scarlet Woman and Her Scarlet Cord"), but something new struck my mind in this latest discussion.

God told Abraham his descendants would not receive their land inheritance for another 400 years because "the iniquity of the Amorite is not yet full" (Gen 15.13–16). The people of Canaan, the Promised Land, were not yet so wicked that God was ready to destroy them, but the time was coming.

If there is a Bible definition for "total depravity" perhaps that is it: "when their iniquity is full." That had happened before in the book of Genesis—to Sodom in Genesis 19, and to the whole world in Genesis 6 when God saw that "every inten-

tion of the thoughts of [man's] heart was only evil continually"
(v 5), another fine definition for total depravity, and the only
way that could possibly be a Biblical doctrine.

Both times God brought about a complete destruction—except for a tiny remnant that we can count on our fingers in each
instance. That means that when God finally brought the Israelites into their land, the Canaanites' iniquity was "full" and
those people must have been every bit as wicked as the people
of Sodom and the world in general in Noah's day.

Yet right in the middle of Jericho, the first city to be con-
quered, a harlot believed in Jehovah God. *A harlot.* Would you
have bothered speaking to her if she were your neighbor, much
less invited her to a Bible study? But she outshone even the
people of God in a way that made God take notice of her.

Thirty-eight years before, when those first 12 spies came
back from their scouting expedition in Numbers 13, ten of them,
the vast majority, gave a fearful report. Look at the words they
used: "we are not able;" "they are stronger than us." Look at
the words Rahab used when she spoke to the two later spies: "I
know the Lord has given you the land;" "our hearts melted and
there was no spirit left in any man...because the Lord your God
he is God." The earlier Israelites raised "a loud cry," "wept all
night," and "grumbled against Moses and Aaron" (Num 14.1–4).
Rahab sent the spies safely on their way and hung a scarlet cord
in her window, patiently waiting for the deliverance promised by
two men she had never seen before in her life, but whose God
she had grown to believe in with all her heart. The difference is
startling. If you didn't know anything but their words and actions, which would you think were children of God?

And a woman like this lived in a place determined for destruction because its iniquity was "full," plying a trade we de-
spise, living a life of moral degradation as a matter of course.

Who lives in your neighborhood? What kind of lives do they lead? Rahab had heard about the God of Israel for forty years (Josh 2.10), assuming she was that old—if not, then all her life. Have your neighbors heard about your God? Have they seen Him in your actions, in your interactions, and in your absolute assurance that He is and that He cares for you, even when life deals you a blow?

Do your words sound like the faithless Israelites' or like the faithful prostitute's? Would God transplant you out of the weeds into the herb garden, or dig you up and throw you out among the thorns and nettles where a useless plant belongs?

Don't count on the fact that you aren't a harlot.

Two men went up into the temple to pray, one a Pharisee and the other a tax collector. The Pharisee, standing by himself, prayed thus: 'God, I thank you that I am not like other men, extortioners, unjust, adulterers, or even like this tax collector. I fast twice a week; I give tithes of all that I get.' But the tax collector, standing far off, would not even lift up his eyes to heaven, but beat his breast, saying, 'God, be merciful to me, a sinner!' I tell you, this man went down to his house justified, rather than the other. For everyone who exalts himself will be humbled, but the one who humbles himself will be exalted."

Luke 18.10–14

41. Picking Blackberries

For the past few years wild blackberries have been rare. The vines are there, full of their painful and aggravatingly sticky thorns, but the fruit dries up before it can fully ripen. First the drought of the late 90s, and then the following dry years of this regular weather cycle of wet and dry have meant that when the time is right, usually early to mid-June, there is nothing to pick. The few that might have survived are devoured quickly by the birds.

This year Lucas found some on a nearby service road, and Keith picked enough for one cobbler for the first time in years. Probably because it has been awhile, I think that was the best blackberry cobbler we ever had. Maybe next year I can make jelly too.

Blackberries are a lot of trouble. The thorns seem like they reach out and grab you. I have often come home with bloody hands and torn clothing—you *never* wear anything you might wear elsewhere when you pick blackberries. But that is not the half of it.

You must also spray yourself and your long-sleeved shirt prodigiously with an insect repellent, and tuck the cuffs of your long pants into your socks. No matter how hot the weather, you must be covered. Without these measures chiggers will find their way in and you will be revisiting your time in the woods far longer and in more unpleasant ways than you wish. Ticks are also a problem. Make sure you pick with someone you don't mind checking you over after you get back home, especially your hair. More than once I have had a tick crawl out of my mop of curls several hours later.

Finally, you must always carry a big stick or a pistol. I prefer pistols because you don't have to get quite as close to the snake to kill it. Birds love blackberries, and snakes like birds, so they often sit coiled under the canes waiting for their meals to fly in. Keith has killed more than one rattlesnake while picking wild blackberries.

Because of all this, since I have Keith, I seldom pick blackberries any more—I let him do it for both of us. Especially since I stand for hours in a hot kitchen afterward, it seems a fair division of labor. When I am making jelly, straining that hot juice through cheesecloth to catch the plenteous seeds and ladling that hot syrupy liquid into hot jars isn't much easier than picking them. But wild blackberries are worth all the trouble. Their scent is sweet and heady and their taste, especially in homemade jellies, almost exotic. The purple hands, teeth, and tongue blackberry lovers wind up with are worth it too. If all you have ever had is commercially grown blackberries and store bought blackberry jelly, you really don't know what they taste like.

Why is it that I can make myself go to all this trouble for something good to eat, and then throw away something far more valuable because "it's not worth it?" Why does teasing my taste buds matter more to me than saving my soul? How many spiritual delicacies have I missed out on because it wasn't worth the trouble?

Serious Bible study can be tedious, but isn't having the Word of God coming instantly to mind when I really need it worth it? When I have taken the time to explore deeply instead of the superficial knowledge most have, isn't it great in the middle of a sermon or Bible class, to suddenly have another passage spring to life right before my mental eyes? "So that's what that means!" is a eureka moment that is nearly incomparable. And while increased knowledge does not necessarily mean increased faith, faith without knowledge is a sham. *Faith comes by hearing and hearing by the word of God* (Rom 10.17). The more scripture you know, the stronger your faith because the more you know about what God has done for us, the more you appreciate it and want to show that appreciation by the service you willingly give.

So many other things we miss out on because we don't want to go to the trouble—cultivating an active prayer life, socializing with brothers and sisters in the faith, helping a new Christian grow, serving the community we live in simply because we care—while at the same time we go to all sorts of trouble for earthly pleasures—sitting in the hot sun on a hard bench amid crude, rowdy people to watch a ball game; searching for a parking space for hours then walking ten blocks in high heels for a favorite meal at a downtown restaurant; standing in long lines at an amusement park, while someone else's ice cream melts on your shirt, and at the same time juggling your own handfuls of fast food, cameras, and tickets, and trying to keep up with rambunctious children. All these things are "worth it." Did you ever ask yourself, "Worth what?" And how long did that pleasure, or whatever your answer is, last?

I would never go to the same amount of trouble for rhubarb that I do for blackberries. That doesn't mean I don't like rhubarb—I make a pretty good strawberry rhubarb cobbler. But rhubarb cannot match blackberries. Spiritually, we too often settle for rhubarb instead of blackberries. You can always tell the ones who don't "settle"—the "purple" fingers from handling the Word of God, and the "purple" teeth and tongues from taking it in on a daily basis and living a life as His servant, give them away.

As for the rich in this present age, charge them not to be haughty, nor to set their hopes on the uncertainty of riches, but on God, **who richly provides us with everything to enjoy.** *They are to do good, to be rich in good works, to be generous and ready to share, thus storing up treasure for themselves as a good foundation for the future,* **so that they may take hold of that which is truly life.**

1 Timothy 6.17–19

42. Boundary Lines

When we first moved onto this land, no one else lived on the parcels anywhere around us. Everyone else bought for the investment and planned to sell later, and with the titles unclear (except for ours) the plots remained empty for a long time. With no fences in place, the boys literally had their own version of the Hundred Acre Woods to play in.

When the first hard rains showed us how the land around here drained, and that we would soon be washed away if something weren't done, the owners to the north of us plowed a ditch along that side to help us out. It was required by law, but they were compliant and even stopped to make sure we were satisfied before their rented equipment went back to the store. Yes, we were. The ditch worked fine and we stayed dry.

We assumed the ditch ran right along the northern edge of the property and used all the land up to it for our garden, for our yard, for flower beds, even for a post to hold guywires for our antenna. When the land around us began to sell and people moved in, we finally had to put up a fence. Imagine our surprise when we discovered that we had been using as much as five feet more land along the north boundary than was actually ours. But of course, the surveyors were correct. They had sighted along the boundary markers, white posts set on all four corners of our five plus acres. I even had to dig up half of a lily bed one morning and transplant them elsewhere so they could put the fence along the correct line.

The Israelites were aware of boundaries and the landmarks that outlined them. "You shall not move your neighbor's landmark, which the men of old have set, in the inheritance that you will hold in the land that the LORD your God is giving you to possess (Deut 19.14). It was a matter of honesty and integrity. "'Cursed be anyone who moves his neighbor's landmark.' And all the people shall say, 'Amen.'" (Deut 27.17). And this is just talking about land. Imagine if someone moved a landmark that showed something even more important than that.

"The princes of Judah have become like those who move the landmark…" (Hos 5.10). The wicked kings of God's people had blurred the lines between right and wrong, between good and evil. The standard became which will make me wealthier or more important among my peers, rather than which is right in the eyes of God? Which is more convenient, which is easier, which do I like the best, which appeals to my lusts? All of these have been used to move the boundaries of right and wrong in people's lives for thousands of years. When the government does it too, we have an instant excuse. After all, it's not against the law, is it?

Do you think it hasn't happened to us? What do you accept now that you would never have accepted thirty years ago because you knew that the Bible said it was wrong? Now people come along and tell you the Bible is a book of myths or the Bible only means what you want it to mean. They have moved the landmark, and many have accepted it.

God does not move landmarks. What He says goes—then and now. He may have changed the rituals we perform in each dispensation, but basic morality—right and wrong—has not and will not change. Even Jesus used the argument, "But from the beginning it was not so…" (Matt 19.8).

We can move the landmarks all we want, but we will still

wind up on the Devil's property, and God will know the difference, whether we accept it or not.

> *Do not move an ancient landmark or enter the fields of the fatherless, for their Redeemer is strong; he will plead their cause against you.*

Proverbs 23.10–11

43. Danger in the Hedgerow

A long time ago we lived near a man who raised a little livestock. He had a sow down the fence line from us, and one summer morning we woke to find piglets rooting their way through our yard, trying to find mama. Mama was too big to get under the pen, but the babies weren't. After that we kept tabs on those piglets, and the boys, who were about 6 and 4, loved going to see them. Baby animals, as a general rule, are cute—even pigs.

One evening I stuck my head out the door and hollered extra loudly, "Dinner!" because I knew that's where they were. Keith said they started back immediately, Nathan on his shoulders, and Lucas walking along side. About halfway back he swapped boys, and told Nathan to run on ahead and wash his hands. As he watched, Nathan ran along the sandy path toward our driveway, then veered to the left instead of to the right toward the house. Immediately his father yelled, 'What did I tell you to do?!" and Nathan instantly changed his direction and ran for the house without even a backward look.

As he approached the deep shade of the drive himself, Keith felt an inch tall. Nathan's tricycle was off to the left, parked in the hedgerow by our chicken pen. That's what he had been headed for because his father had taught him to always put up his tricycle.

He put Lucas down on the ground and sent him on into the house as he went for the tricycle himself, to put it up for his younger son, who had only been trying to obey his father in all things. Just as he got there, a gray-green cottonmouth as thick as a bike tire tube charged from the bushes. Keith was able to grab a shovel in time and kill it.

Imagine if he had been a four year old. Would he have seen the snake in time? Would he have even known to be on the look out as one should here in the north Florida piney woods? Cottonmouths are not shy—not only will they charge, they will change direction and come after you. A snake that size could easily have struck above Nathan's waist, and at only forty pounds he was probably dead on his feet.

Now let me ask you this—does your child obey you instantly? Or do you have to argue, threaten, bribe, or cajole him into doing what you tell him to do? Do you think it doesn't matter? The world is filled with dangerous things, even if you don't live where I do—traffic, electricity, deep water, high drop offs— predators. If you don't teach him instant obedience, you could be responsible for his injury or death some day—*you*, because you didn't teach him to obey. Because you thought it wasn't that important. Because you thought it would make him hate you. Because you thought it made you sound mean. Or dozens of other excuses.

We put our boys in child car seats before it was required by law. We actually had other people ask us, "How do you get him to sit in the seat?" Excuse me? Isn't it funny that when the law started requiring it, those parents figured it out? Not getting in trouble with the law was evidently more important to them than the welfare of their children.

The hedgerows don't go away when your child grows up. In fact, they become even more dangerous if you haven't taught him as you should have. Isn't it sad when the elders of the church have to nag people to get them to do one simple thing for the betterment of the church or the visitors whose souls they are supposed to care about, like sitting somewhere besides the two back pews? Those are probably the same people who as children had to be begged to obey their parents.

Do you want to know what someone was like as a child? I can show you the ones who threw tantrums; they're the ones who threaten to leave if things aren't done their way. I can point out the ones who wouldn't share their toys; they won't give up anything now either, especially not their "rights." The snake in the hedgerow has bitten them, and this time it poisoned their souls, not their bodies.

Look around you Sunday morning. Decide which of those adults you want your children to be like when they grow up. It doesn't happen automatically. It happens when loving parents *work hard*, sometimes enduring a whole lot of unpleasantness and even criticism, to mold their children into disciples of the Lord.

Danger hides in the hedgerows. Make sure your child's soul stays safe.

*Now Adonijah [David's son and] the son of Haggith exalted himself, saying, "**I** will be king." And he prepared for himself chariots and horsemen, and fifty men to run before him. **His father had never at any time displeased him by asking, "Why have you done thus and so?"***

1 Kings 1.5–6

*On that day I will fulfill against Eli all that I have spoken concerning his house, from beginning to end. And I declare to him that I am about to punish his house forever, for the iniquity that **he knew**, because his sons were blaspheming God, **and he did not restrain them.***

1 Samuel 3.12–13

44. Lord of the Flies

We had a terrible time with gnats this past summer. Despite our automatic atomizer, a dozen swarmed the lights at night and several buzzed us during dinner. So I looked up the reproductive process of gnats and found out why. We live in a veritable breeding ground—standing water (water buckets for the dogs), damp landscaping (mulch in the flower beds and more rain this year than any in the past ten), food (a large vegetable garden, a blueberry patch, and grape vines), and, ahem, animal residue—we live in the country, it's everywhere.

So keeping the doors and windows shut should fix the problem, right? No, they breed in garbage cans too. When you live in a small rural county there is no weekly pickup. You must carry your own garbage and trash to the dump. To minimize the number of trips we put all the flammable items in a paper bag to burn in the "burn barrel" onsite, and the wet garbage in the kitchen can until it fills enough to empty it into the one outside. That means our kitchen can is probably emptied less often than yours because there is no paper trash "filler," and that means plenty of time for any gnats that whiz in a door as we enter or leave to lay eggs and hatch. I have tried spraying it every morning with insecticide, but even that does not seem to help.

I've heard it all my life: you can catch more flies with honey than with vinegar. Imagine my surprise to find out you can catch quite a few flies with vinegar after all.

I read it in a cooking magazine. Most gnats are fruitflies. If you are having trouble with gnats in your kitchen, fill a small dish with vinegar, squeeze a drop of two of dishwashing liquid on it and set it out where you have the most gnats. What interests a fruitfly is the vinegars formed in the rotten fruit, and that bowl of vinegar spells "rotten fruit" to their little sensory receptors. Because of the surface tension on water, a fruitfly can land and not sink, but that drop of dishwashing liquid breaks the tension. They land and sink, drowning immediately.

I put one of these dishes out one day and an hour later found 18 little black specks lying on the bottom, never to buzz in my house again. Now, every summer, I have two or three custard cups of apple cider vinegar lying around my house, and far fewer gnats than ever before.

One of the cups sits on the window sill next to the chair that overlooks the bird feeder. That bird feeder attracts more than its fair share of gnats in the summer too, and I have a suspicion that most of the gnats in the house sneak through the cracks around that window. The screen is gone so I can see the birds better and the double window is up a foot so I have a place for my coffee cup on the sill. That lack of triple protection means they can get in easier than anywhere else in the house except an open door.

So the other afternoon I sat down to rest a bit after canning a bushel of tomatoes. Keith was emptying the residual garbage pails of skins and seeds, and dumping the heavy pots of boiling water outside so the house wouldn't heat up yet more from the steam. I had just replaced the vinegar in the dish a few minutes before.

A gnat suddenly buzzed my face and I shooed it away. He came back, but this time he headed straight for the window. "Aha!" I thought. If I just sat still I could see how it actually happened. It was a real life lesson.

He had gotten "wind" of the vinegar somehow and flew over to check it out at a prudent distance of eight or ten inches, which is several thousand times the body length of a gnat I imagine, and was certainly safe. He flew away, but within a few seconds he was back. This time he flew a little closer, maybe half the distance he had before.

That happened several times with the gnat coming in closer and closer on each pass. Finally, he landed on the window sill a couple of inches from the custard cup. I could just imagine him sitting there tensed up and waiting for something to happen, then finally relaxing as he discovered that whatever danger he had imagined wasn't there.

He flew again, but not away. This time he hovered over the cup, doing figure eights two or three inches above the surface of the vinegar. Then he landed on the lip of the custard cup. At that point I imagine the fumes from the fresh vinegar were nearly intoxicating. All that rotten fruit right down there for the taking, and besides, he had never had trouble before landing on a piece of bruised, decaying fruit, and this one was obviously an apple, one of the best.

So he flew yet again, circling closer and closer to the surface. "Now," he must have thought as he landed on what he was sure was a solid chunk of overripe Macintosh, or Jonathan, or Red Rome, and promptly sank into the vinegar. He didn't even wiggle—it was over that fast, his drowning in what he thought was safe, in a place where nothing bad had ever happened to him before.

It works this way for humans too, you know. What are you hovering over today?

Look not thou upon the wine when it is red, When it sparkles in the cup, When it goes down smoothly: At the last it bites like a serpent, And stings like an adder.

Proverbs 23.31–32

Thorns and snares are in the way of the perverse: He who keeps his soul shall be far from them.

Proverbs 22.5

45. Look Under the Pillow

A few mornings back Keith and I took our last cup of coffee to the carport and sat in our nylon lounge chairs, the kind with the attached pillow you can flip over the back if you do not care to use it. We did use them, both of us, and leaned back, watching the mockingbird flit back and forth to its nest in the bloom-laden rose trellis and the hummingbirds guard their two feeders like Fort Knox. A couple of squirrels ran along the "highway," a route they use every day from one live oak top to another, down the limbs and across the fence. Off in the distance a hawk screamed, a rooster crowed, and a wild turkey gobbled. Occasionally we flipped a treat out for Chloe to chase. It was still the middle of spring, cool and bugless, humidity low for a Florida morning, low enough that the scent of jasmine reached us from the vine 75 feet down the drive.

After twenty minutes or so, we got up to start our morning. As soon as Keith stood, a snake slithered out from under his pillow, down the back of the chair and dropped onto the carport. Our chairs are only six inches apart. If that thing had stuck its head out between us from under the pillow, judging by the roar when he saw it, Keith might have had a heart attack, and I might still be running. Talk about "Flight Paths"—I would have made a good one.

Guess what we do every morning now? That's right. We flip those pillows back and look under them *before* we sit down.

People say habits are hard to break. We didn't have a bit of trouble breaking ourselves of sitting down before we looked. Depends upon the motivation, I guess. Maybe that's why we have such a hard time breaking ourselves of sinful habits—we enjoy them too much, or we just don't think they are that important.

From another perspective, we didn't have a bit of trouble creating a new habit either. Same reason—motivation. I really do not want to think about a snake lying under the pillow I am leaning my head against, or the possibility of it slithering down my back, do you?

So why can't we make new habits to rid ourselves of that besetting sin in our lives? Can't I learn to pray for self-control before I leave the house when I know I have trouble behind the wheel? Can't I learn to recite a few passages about longsuffering and kindness just before I walk into a meeting with that particularly obnoxious colleague? Can't I learn to avoid situations that I know will tempt me instead of purposefully putting my soul in harm's way? Of course I can, if I care enough, if I believe God would want me to do so, if I think of Him instead of me and my stubborn will.

And, if I believe that Satan is real, that he is out there trying to find a way to make me fall. He is, you know. He is right under that pillow, waiting for you to sit down without a care in the world and lean your vulnerable neck back into reach of his fangs.

Change a habit today. LOOK! *before* you sit down.

But put on the Lord Jesus Christ, and make no provision for the flesh, to gratify its desires.

Romans 13.14

46. Garden Suppers

This is one of our favorite times of the year—the garden is booming and dinner will always be a treat of things we can only enjoy now, when the vegetables are truly "vine-ripened" and the price is perfect—just a lot of sweat.

One night we will have stuffed bell peppers in a fresh tomato sauce with green beans on the side. The next we will have eggplant parmigiana with a squash casserole on the side. Later in the week it will be a country veggie plate of butterbeans, sliced tomatoes, roasted corn, fried okra, and a big wedge of cornbread. Pasta night will feature a fresh tomato sauce with fresh oregano and feta cheese or a simple cherry tomato sauce with fresh basil. Then there will be the times we try something new, like today's grilled eggplant and red onion sandwich on a toasted multi-grain bun with lemon aioli and a big slice of tomato plus pita chips and baba ghanoush (a dip of grilled eggplant and tahini) on the side. As the rest of the vegetables die off, we will still have the Italian plum tomatoes and enjoy a pizza with homemade crust and tomato sauce, plus a few late season peppers and some Italian sausage. A few nights later, we will do the same thing, but fold it over and make a calzone out of it with the sauce on the side. Yes, this is one of our favorite times of the year.

But now we are seeing that it will have to end sometime in the near future. Maybe it's the heat, maybe it's our age, maybe it's a combination of the two, but all this good food isn't worth sacrificing our health for, much less our lives. Someday soon we will have to buy canned and frozen foods at the store like everyone else instead of using the preserved items we have labored over for three months every year.

Which all serves to remind us of what we have lost and why. "By the sweat of your face you shall eat bread, till you return to the ground, for out of it you were taken; for you are dust, and to dust you shall return" (Gen 3.19).

We sweat a lot over this garden. Some days I think it is watered more by us than the rain. That is as it should be, for sin deserves far worse punishment than that and every one of us has participated in it. It is by God's mercy that we plant in the spring when we have a cool breeze and a sun that is not directly over us. That same mercy grants us a salvation we do not deserve, and the help to make it through a life we have all but ruined from the beginning. Why should we expect a perfect life now? Why should we expect that things will always turn out right? Someone has not been reading the same Bible I have. It is grace that promises us that there is a perfect place in the future. Don't look upon that hope with ingratitude because you cannot have it now. We have only ourselves to blame.

But in the midst of the toil, the sweat, the thorns and thistles and weeds, we enjoy a few weeks of some of the best meals in the world—not gourmet feasts, not something concocted by a celebrity chef—but the plain and simple fare that comes straight from the ground and reminds us of the provision God has made "for the just and the unjust," not because He had to, but because He wanted to. It also reminds us of the garden we will return to someday, and never have to leave again. If you don't have your own garden, head to the farmers' market this week and remind yourselves that God still loves us. This is the way it is supposed to be, and it can be again. It's up to you whether you get to enjoy it.

> *Therefore, just as sin came into the world through one man, and death through sin, and so death spread to all men because all sinned. ... But the free gift is not like the trespass. For if many died through one man's trespass, much more have the grace of God and the free gift by the grace of that one man Jesus Christ abounded for many. ... For if, because of one man's trespass, death reigned through that one man, much more will those who receive the abundance of grace and the free gift of righteousness reign in life through the one man Jesus Christ.*

Romans 5.12, 15, 17

47. A January Daisy

It had been unseasonably warm for a few weeks, so warm the blueberries had begun to bloom. Not good in January, for up here in North Florida we could be sure more frosts and freezes awaited us. But there was nothing we could do about it, so we went on about our business, and one morning as I pulled myself along with the trekking poles, walking Chloe around the property, I suddenly came upon a yellow daisy right in the middle of a patch of green grass, another product of the warm spell. It sat there only four inches off the ground and a little scraggly. Still, it made me smile.

Then I got a virus and found myself in the sickbed for over a week. Finally, the chest congestion drained, the ears stopped aching, and the nose could suddenly breathe again, so after one more day of recovery, I took Chloe on another walk. As I came around the blueberries I saw it again, still hanging on in spite of the now cooler temperatures—and once again I smiled.

I suddenly wondered if we aren't supposed to be like that lone little daisy out in the world. Do we make anyone smile? Or are we just like everyone else, hurrying along, consumed with ourselves and our business, impatient, or even angry, with the ones who get in our way and slow us down? We have an obligation to others we pass along the way.

"You shall not see your brother's donkey or his ox fallen down by the way and ignore them. You shall help him to lift them up again." (Deut 22.4)

That one is pretty easy, we say. Who wouldn't stop for a brother on the side of the road whose donkey (or car) was broken down? Keith stood by the side of the road next to a disabled car one night, and watched brother after brother pass him on the way to the gospel meeting that was being held just a mile or two down the highway, so don't be too sure of yourself.

Yet the law also says this: "If you meet your *enemy's* ox or his donkey going astray, you shall bring it back to him. If you see the donkey of *one who hates you* lying down under its burden, you shall refrain from leaving him with it; you shall rescue it with him" (Exod 23.4–5). How many of us feel any obligation at all to bear the burden of an enemy, or just a stranger?

Let's not make it one of those situations where we excuse ourselves by talking about crime and good sense. How about this? Did you make the cashier's day a little brighter or a little tougher when you went through the line this morning? Did you stop and help the harried young mother who dropped her grocery list and sent coupons scattering across the aisle, or did you sigh loudly at the inconvenience of her, her cart, and her three rowdy children because you were in a hurry to get home? Did you make small talk with the waitress who poured your coffee, or did you treat her like a piece of furniture? Did you slow down and make room for the car that cut you off in traffic, or did you talk and gesticulate and lay on the horn long enough for someone to think we were in an air raid? Did you make *anyone* smile this morning?

"At my first defense, no one came to stand by me, but all deserted me," Paul said in 2 Timothy 4.16. Nearly impossible to imagine, isn't it? Yet the night before Keith was scheduled to testify in a trial where we knew the only defense was to try to discredit him, a brother decided he needed to call him up and castigate him for an imagined slight, something that he had simply misunderstood. When all we can think about is ourselves instead of bearing one another's burdens (Gal 6.2), instead of helping the weak (1 Thes 5.14), instead of comforting one another, (2 Cor 1.4), that's exactly what happens.

Yes, we get comfort from God, but guess how that often happens? "But God, who comforts the downcast, comforted us by the coming of Titus" (2 Cor 7.6). We are the comfort that God gives. We are the help that He provides. It's up to us to pay attention and think of someone besides ourselves.

Today, be a January daisy, something lovely and unexpected in the life of someone who needs it, whether a brother, or an enemy, or just a stranger. Make someone smile.

> *Anxiety in a man's heart weighs him down, but a good word makes him glad.*
>
> Proverbs 12.25

> *Gracious words are like a honeycomb, sweetness to the soul and health to the body.*
>
> Proverbs 16.24

> *I rejoice at the coming of Stephanas and Fortunatus and Achaicus… for they refreshed my spirit….*
>
> 1 Corinthians 16.17–18

48. As the Butterfly Goes

My big flower bed on the south side of the shed attracts butterflies by the score. Every day I see both white and yellow sulfurs, tiny blue hairstreaks, huge brown and yellow swallowtails, and glorious orange monarchs and viceroys flitting from bloom to bloom. Sometimes it's hard to tell where the bloom stops and the butterfly begins amid all those big yellow black-eyed Susans, multicolored zinnias, and purple petunias.

But have you ever watched a butterfly? If you and I decided to go somewhere the way a butterfly goes, it would take all day to get there. We have a saying: "as the crow flies," meaning a straight line course. A butterfly couldn't fly a straight line no matter how hard it tried—it would always fail the state trooper's sobriety test.

Some of us live our spiritual lives like butterflies. We seem to think that waking up in the morning and allowing life to just "happen" is the way to go. No wonder we don't grow. No wonder we fail again and again at the same temptations. No wonder we don't know more about the Word of God this year than last, and no wonder we can't stand the trials of faith.

Some folks think that going to church is the plan. That's why their neighbors would be surprised to find out they are Christians—Sunday is their only day of service. Others refuse to acknowledge any weakness they need to work on. It rankles their pride to admit they need to improve on anything, and because they won't admit anything specific, they never do improve.

Some folks make their life decisions with no consideration at all for their spiritual health, or the good of the kingdom. The stuff of this life matters the most, and only after that do they give the spiritual a thought, if at all, and it is to be dismissed if it means anything untoward for their physical comfort, convenience, status, or wealth.

The only plan they have for their children is their physical welfare—how they will do in school, where they will go to college, what career they will pursue. They must get their schoolwork, but their parents don't even know what they are studying in Bible classes, much less make sure they get their lessons. It's too much trouble to take them to spiritual gatherings of other young Christians. And have you seen how much those camps cost?! Probably less than a year's worth of cell phone service and much less than the car they buy those same kids.

Where is the plan for this family's spiritual growth? Where is their devotion to a God they claim as Lord? If their children do end up faithful, it will be in spite of these parents, not because of them.

God expects us to have a plan. The writer of the seventeenth psalm had one. "I have purposed that my mouth will not transgress," he says in verse 3, and then later, "I have avoided the ways of the violent, my steps have held fast to your paths," (4b–5a). He made a vow and he kept it. He mapped his life out to stay away from evil and on the road to his Father.

How are you doing as you fly through life—and it does fly, people! Are you flitting here and there, around one bush and over another, out of the flower bed entirely once in awhile, then back in for a quick sip of nectar before heading off in whichever direction the wind blows? Or do you have a plan, a map to get you past the pitfalls with as little danger as possible, to the necessary stops for revival and refreshing, but then straight back on the road to your next life?

Do you know what the term social butterfly means? It's someone who flits from group to group. Perhaps not so much now, but originally the term was one of ridicule. I wonder what God would think of a spiritual butterfly who has no focus on the spiritual things of this life, but flits from one thing to other and always on a carnal whim rather than a spiritual one. I wonder if He would decide that butterfly wouldn't be able to appreciate an eternity of spiritual things either.

> *...And [Barnabas] exhorted them all to remain faithful to the Lord **with steadfast purpose**, for he was a good man, full of the Holy Spirit and of faith....*

> Acts 11.23–24

49. Old Trees

Despite my trekking poles, I still have an occasional stumble as I walk Chloe around the property in the mornings. Trees have a way of shedding limbs, especially in a brisk spring breeze, of pelting the ground with pine cones that roll beneath the feet, and showering the ground with slick leaves and needles. All of those things hide holes and depressions that can turn an ankle. I haven't fallen in a while, thanks to these sturdy fiberglass poles, but it's still a little dangerous out there for someone with limited vision.

Most of those trees are ancient by human standards. After watching a live oak we planted grow from a one foot "stick" to a fifteen foot sapling in 20 years, I know the ones that spread over our house, so large it would take four people to hold hands around them, must be closing in on the century mark. The wonderful thing about those trees, especially in this climate, is the shade. With limbs stretching out thirty to forty feet, and dense foliage, the temperature beneath them can be ten to fifteen degrees cooler than in the sun.

Trees, then, can be either a source of comfort or a hindrance. On occasion, a tree has deposited a limb right in the middle of our driveway, and there are few places along its length where you can drive out of the road around a blockage. The older the trees, in fact, the bigger the problem they can cause. We pray constantly, especially in hurricane season, that one of those thousand pound limbs will not fall on the house.

As I become older, I realize the same is true of me. The aged can be a source of strength, wisdom, and encouragement. God surely intended that to be the case. *Wisdom is with the aged, and understanding in length of days* (Job 12.12). Unfortunately we can also be a source of discouragement and a hindrance to spiritual life. Instead of gaining wisdom, some of us store up hurts and slights, many of them magnified through the years or even imagined. Instead of learning the lessons of life, we become bitter. Instead of maturing and reaching out to others, we continue, as we so often did when young, to demand attention.

On this rural property we have learned through the years which trees are most helpful and which are most damaging. I step over far more pine limbs than oak, but even among those stately hardwoods are some we have learned to beware of. A water oak will drop branches on your house or your car or your power lines, will in fact, be as likely as a pine tree to completely fall over.

It may not seem fair, but if you are a young person looking for a mentor, you must, as Jesus said, judge people by their fruits. If you find yourself hearing nothing but the negative, you are taking shelter under the wrong tree.

If you, like me, are heading toward that label "elderly," you need to think about the shelter you offer the young. I will be judged by "every idle word." Certainly around the young and impressionable, around those who may look to me for wisdom and advice, I must be careful not to cause them to stumble in their confidence by casting off branches of discouragement. I must not block their pathway to spiritual growth with selfish resentment about the past. I certainly must not squash their zeal with cynicism about either the world or their brethren. If ever there is a time when our choice of words is crucial, it is old age, when the young look to us for advice and help.

We cannot help becoming old. But we can all determine how we will act as one of those older "trees." What did Jesus say about branches that were unfruitful? Do we really think he will do less to us if we fail in our purpose as the older, wiser heads?

O God, from my youth you have taught me, and I still proclaim your wondrous deeds. So even to old age and gray hairs, O God, do not forsake me, until I proclaim your might to another generation, your power to all those to come.

Psalm 71.17–18

50. The Fury of the Storm

Summer thunderstorms are nothing unusual in Florida. Even when we don't have a hurricane, we can count on dark skies, roiling clouds, strong winds, and heavy downpours almost every afternoon from June through September. This summer seems to have been worse than usual.

Just in the past four days we have had two storms that knocked the power out for a total of seven hours, with two plus inches falling in an hour's time. In fact, this last time we had an inch and a half in thirty minutes flat. The water ran down from the top of the hill in a river around the house and down to the creek just past the boundary fence. The wind blew the rain in nearly horizontal sheets, leaving standing water an inch deep on the covered carport, and the screened porch floor wet to the wall of the house. The wind blew in gusts that twisted fifteen foot long pine limbs off the trees—green limbs, not rotten ones. Smaller limbs flew by as we watched, almost as thick as the rainwater. The lightning was loud and close and almost constant. When I stepped inside and saw the power was out I was not really surprised. This was one angry storm.

And suddenly I thought, "This was the kind of rain Noah lived through." God was angry. He would not have sent a gentle patter of raindrops on that gopher wood roof. His wrath would have been obvious in the gusty winds tearing roofs off houses and branches off trees. He would have vented his anger in the boom of thunder rolling over the hills, hills that slowly and inevitably disappeared under the waves. That last storm we had scared me just a little; I bet the one Noah endured for forty days was terrifying.

And we need to be terrified too. An angry God is not the God we want to face on judgment day. Do not let the world, and sometimes even the brethren, blur your view of an irate God who cannot countenance sin. You need that picture to keep you straight sometimes, and so do I. It's too easy to think, "This is no big deal; God won't mind this once; God is a God of mercy," and forget the God of wrath and vengeance. Don't let anyone turn "fear" into nothing more than respect. You can love someone and fear them too. Anyone who had a godly father knows that. Don't let them lie to you and steal your soul by telling you otherwise.

By the end of summer I am ready for a calm fall. I want sunny days and gentle breezes. I am sure that's what we want from God too, but just as those storms do good for this land—replenishing the water table and keeping the tropical plants green—remembering the stormy wrath of God can do your soul good too. Don't forget it.

Therefore thus says the Lord GOD: I will make a stormy wind break out in my wrath, and there shall be a deluge of rain in my anger, and great hailstones in wrath to make a full end.

Ezekiel 13.13

But sexual immorality and all impurity or covetousness must not even be named among you, as is proper among saints. Let there be no filthiness nor foolish talk nor crude joking, which are out of place, but instead let there be thanksgiving. For you may be sure of this, that everyone who is sexually immoral or impure, or who is covetous (that is, an idolater), has no inheri-

tance in the kingdom of Christ and God. Let no one deceive you with empty words, for because of these things the wrath of God comes upon the sons of disobedience.

Ephesians 5.3–6

51 Just a Bunch of Stems

My little boys used to bring me bouquets all the time. Sometimes it was Queen Anne's lace. Sometimes it was a bright blue spiderwort. Sometimes it was a rain lily or a stem of pink clover. Sometimes it was just a dandelion bloom. All of these are wildflowers, what any suburban lawn grower would call "weeds." Yet I put them all in vases of various sizes because they were all precious to me. My little fellows had no idea the difference between domesticated flowers and wildflowers. All they knew was "flowers," and out here in the country we are surrounded by them.

But even they would never have gathered a bunch of them, ripped off the blooms and handed me a fistful of stems. The problem with religion today, including some of my own brothers and sisters, is they value the stems and not the flowers.

A few months ago someone told me how listening to a certain teacher had made his day so much better. I anxiously awaited the lesson he had heard, but he never once said a word about the content. All I heard was the teacher's name, at least three times, and how that *person* had made his day better. What he had done was throw away the flower and put the empty stem in a vase of water to admire.

I understand having favorite speakers and teachers. Nothing makes me happier than to hear someone compliment my husband and my sons. But none of them teach for the glory. They teach to help people. If all people remember is their names, then they haven't been much help, have they?

If I can't tell you what a person taught me, did I learn anything, or was I just entertained for a few brief moments? One of my favorite teachers isn't much of an entertainer, but I always go away with a new way of looking at things, even things I have been looking at for decades now. He makes me think, and he makes me see the possibilities. He makes me want to go look at it again myself, and I often do. He makes me examine my life in ways I never have and want to change for the better. Can your favorite speaker do those things, or does he just make you laugh and feel good?

There is absolutely nothing wrong with going to someone for help with your Bible study. God did ordain the role of teachers in spiritual things (Eph 4.11). He meant for us to have brothers and sisters we could go to with questions and problems. Paul told Timothy to pass on what he knew to "faithful men." He told the older to train the younger. But God also holds us individually accountable for what we do with what we hear. "Work out your own salvation," Paul told the Philippians, well after Jesus had already said, "If the blind lead the blind, they shall both fall into the ditch." It is up to each of us to be careful to whom we listen and to examine what they say against the Word (Acts 17.11).

A good teacher doesn't care if s/he receives praise or not—that is not his/her purpose. All s/he does is hold up the Word of God and present it to you. "What is the straw to the wheat?" God asks in Jeremiah 23.28. That word "straw" has several meanings according to Strong's, and one of them is the wheat stalk, or stem. Which is more important, God is saying, the stem or the wheat it holds up?

I knew a man once who nearly tore a church up because he insisted on "his turn" to teach when not only was he a lousy teacher, he didn't even know the Word of God accurately enough to teach it. Clearly, it was all about the glory of teaching to him, and clearly he needed the admonition in Romans 12.3: "For by the grace given to me I say to everyone among you not to think of himself more highly than he ought to think, but to think with sober judgment, each according to the measure of faith that God has assigned."

I know the temptation. So did Paul. "I refrain from [boasting], so that no one may think more of me than he sees in me or hears from me. So to keep me from becoming conceited because of the surpassing greatness of the revelations, a thorn was given me in the flesh, a messenger of Satan to harass me, to keep me from becoming conceited" (2 Cor 12.6–7). It shouldn't matter to me what people say about my speaking or writing. What should matter is how many I reach, how many are helped and encouraged and how many souls are saved. And that is what should matter to those who listen and read too.

And do you know why this is so important? If you value the who above the what, someday, sooner or later, you *will* be deceived into believing a lie. Even good teachers make mistakes, and you might be deceived by an honest error too. That is why James tells us that teachers will receive the "greater condemnation" (3.1). Teaching is a responsibility, and anyone who craves the glory is manifestly unable to handle that burden.

Most of the preachers and teachers I know will tell you the same things I am now. If you want to make me happy, then use what I give you, remember it and grow. Share it with others who might need it. Even if you forget where you got it, just pass the good news along. That is what really matters. Give them a bouquet of flowers, not a handful of stems.

For if anyone thinks he is something, when he is nothing, he deceives himself.

Galatians 6.3

52. Reminiscing

It must be a sign of age. I find myself reminiscing a lot more lately. When we walked the property with Lucas last Thanksgiving we talked more about the past than the present. Certainly more than the future—which for us is suddenly so much smaller than the past.

"Remember the wild myrtles by the fire pit?"

"Yes, we sometimes hung a tarp on the branches so we could scoot under it and have a hot dog roast even in a drizzle."

"Remember the pine tree in the field?"

"Yep. That was first base."

"Remember how small these oak trees used to be?"

"Yes. I used to climb up limbs that are too rotten to trust any longer, what there are left of them."

I remember wondering what it would be like after the boys were grown, when we were living here alone in a quiet house and an empty yard. No more wondering, only remembering.

I have said to more than one who came seeking advice that looking back on our past can be helpful. If you despair at ever becoming the Christian you ought to be, look where you were ten years ago. Can you see any improvement? Can you say to yourself, "I don't act that way now," about anything at all? God meant for us to be encouraged, and I find nothing in the scriptures telling me I can't take a moment every now and then to check my progress and use it as a gauge, both to spur myself on if I see none, and to invigorate my growth with any positive impetus it gives me.

Many times we quote Paul's comment to the Philippians, "Forgetting the things that are behind..." (3.13). In fact, I have heard preachers say we shouldn't think about the past at all. But Paul didn't believe that. He remembered all his life where he started, "the chief of sinners" (1 Tim 1.16). He used that memory to keep himself humble before others and grateful to God for the salvation granted him. It bolstered his faith enough to endure countless hardships and persecutions. As a "chief sinner" he could hardly rail against God for the tortures he suffered when he knew he deserved so much more.

God has always wanted his people to remember the past. I lost count of the passages in Deuteronomy exhorting Israel to remember that they were slaves in a foreign country, and that God loved them enough to deliver them with His mighty hand. Here is a case, though, where the reminding didn't work as it did for Paul. Still, God tried. What is the Passover but a reminder of their deliverance from Egypt? What is the Feast of Tabernacles but a reminder of His care for them in the wilderness? What was the pot of manna in the Ark of the Covenant, the stones on the breastplate of the ephod, and the pile of rocks by the Jordan but the same? "Remember, remember, remember!" God enjoined. It's how we use that memory that makes it right or wrong.

Paul says we are to remember what we used to be. "And such were some of you," he reminds the Corinthians in chapter 6, after listing what we consider the worst sins imaginable. You "were servants of sin" he reminds the Romans (6.17). You once walked "according to the course of this world," "in vanity of mind," "in the desire of the Gentiles," and in a host of other sins too numerous to list (Eph 2.2; 4.17; 1 Pet 4.3; Col 3; Titus 3.) Those memories should spur us on in the same way they prodded Paul. Nothing is too hard to bear, too much to ask, or too difficult to overcome if we remember where we started. Be encouraged by your growth and take heart.

And then this: let your gratitude be always abounding, overflowing, and effusive to a God who loves us in whatever state we find ourselves, as long as that growth continues.

> *Therefore remember that at one time you Gentiles in the flesh, called "the uncircumcision" by what is called the circumcision, which is made in the flesh by hands—remember that you were at that time separated from Christ, alienated from the commonwealth of Israel and strangers to the covenants of promise, having no hope and without God in the world. But now in Christ Jesus you who once were far off have been brought near by the blood of Christ.*

Ephesians 2.11–13

Also by Dene Ward

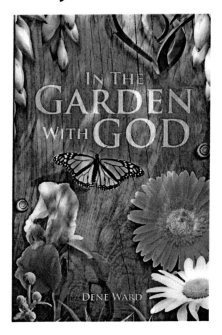

In the Garden with God

Dene Ward and her husband Keith have gardened for nearly 40 years, which has shown her why God's prophets and preachers, including Jesus, used so many references to plants and planting—it's only natural. Join her for a walk in the garden with God. 142 pages. $9.99 (PB)

Flight Paths

A Devotional Guide for your Journey

When encroaching blindness took her music teaching career away, Dene Ward turned her attention to writing. What began as e-mail devotions to some friends grew into a list of hundreds of subscribers. Three hundred sixty-six of those devotions have been assembled to form this daily devotional. Follow her through a year of camping, bird-watching, medical procedures, piano lessons, memories, and more as she uses daily life as a springboard to thought-provoking and character-challenging messages of endurance and faith. 475 pages. $18.99 (PB)

Soul Food

Lessons from Hearth to Heart

Cooking has always been a part of Dene Ward's life. She grew up in a house where they were always feeding someone and followed that same path as a wife and mother. On the table, she has always offered a nourishing meal; she now offers this collection to feed your souls, lessons from her hearth to your heart. 148 pages. $9.99 (PB)

for your journey

DeWard™

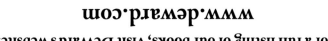

For a full listing of our books, visit DeWard's website:

www.deward.com